BEAT THE ODDS
Blackjack

BEAT THE ODDS
Blackjack

PLAYING PERCENTAGES
WITHOUT COUNTING

G. Phillip Cline

LYLE STUART
Kensington Publishing Corp.
www.kensingtonbooks.com

LYLE STUART BOOKS are published by

Kensington Publishing Corp.
850 Third Avenue
New York, NY 10022

All Kensington titles, imprints, and distributed lines are available at special quantity discounts for bulk purchases for sales promotions, premiums, fund-raising, educational, or institutional use. Special book excerpts or customized printings can also be created to fit specific needs. For details, write or phone the office of the Kensington special sales manager: Kensington Publishing Corp., 850 Third Avenue, New York, NY 10022, attn: Special Sales Department, phone 1-800-221-2647.

Lyle Stuart is a trademark of Kensington Publishing Corp.

First printing: December 2003

10 9 8 7 6 5 4 3 2 1

Printed in the United States of America

ISBN 0-8184-0636-4

DEDICATED

To Teri

My shadow
My gambling buddy
My best friend
My love
My soul mate
My inspiration
My everything

You are always with me

ACKNOWLEDGMENTS

To my three children: Jeff, Greg, and Susan. You all sacrificed a great deal while I was researching this book and making it a reality. For your love, support, and understanding, I am forever grateful. You have all grown into strong, special adults, and I am so very blessed to have you in my life. I love you.

To my father, Albert, for the many sacrifices you have made for me over the years and for the help and love you have given me throughout my life. Thank you.

To my mother, Lois, and in her loving memory. No son could have had a gentler guiding hand throughout his early life than you. I miss you.

I would be remiss if I did not give my special and heartfelt thanks to three very special people:

One was there for me at the beginning of this adventure and gave me her contagious enthusiasm and encouragement to take the first step and write the first page. Thank you, Dr. Elizabeth Latosi-Sawin of Missouri Western State College in Saint Joseph, Missouri.

Next, I wish to acknowledge someone I had not yet met at the beginning of this project, but who was essential for the final, finished product. I believe that if not for her work, caring, and expertise, this book would never have been completed. A very special "thank-you" to Sue Ann Buddin of Diversified Office Services in San Angelo, Texas.

Finally, my thanks to Carla J. Jones of Laser Graphics in San Angelo, Texas, for her great work on the illustrations.

CONTENTS

Preface

Blackjack is truly a fascinating game. You can win a lot of money playing it and you can lose a lot of money playing it.

The key to success at playing blackjack is to become as knowledgeable as you can about it. You must have knowledge of the game, patience, self-control, and good money management to win. Without these four things, you will surely lose. It's just that simple. Set yourself some goals and some limits, both in winning and losing. You will not win every time you play, but with a method that works and that you can believe in, you will win more often than you lose.

The basic strategy used by most players in the game of blackjack was developed and refined from the 1950s to the 1980s by a number of men who wanted to find a definitive way to play the game. In 1956, an article titled "The Optimum Strategy in Blackjack" was published by Roger Baldwin, Wilbert Cantery, Herbert Maisel, and James McDermott. These men demonstrated in their article that, by following their basic playing strategy of when to hit, stand, split, or double-down, a player could reduce the house advantage by almost half (yet still *not* have an advantage *over* the house). MIT Professor Edward O. Thorp took their work a step further and worked out computer simulations of blackjack games and determined that the player would have advantages over the house after certain cards were played. In 1962 he published his findings in a book called *Beat the Dealer*. The success of his book was the impetus for many casinos to change from one-deck games to multideck games in order to thwart his strategy. Julian Braun at IBM further refined the basic strategy using powerful computers, playing millions of hands. He calculated for rule variations at different casinos and came up with a definitive basic strategy, one that could be slightly modified for rule changes. In 1980 he published his results in a book, *How to Play Winning Blackjack*. The basic strategy used by most players today is Braun's with minor variations introduced by other authors since then. This strategy, however, only reduces the house's advantage to 0.5 percent; it does not give the player an advantage over the house. It is also predicated on computer simulations of millions of hands; that means that only over the long run will the odds at the casino match the computer-calculated basic strategy. Considering how badly most people play blackjack, a reduction of the house advantage to 0.5 percent would almost seem like winning—almost.

Let's take a fantasy journey. Let's pretend we are invisible and can hover over a casino floor. We can see everything that is going on at every blackjack table from an overhead view. We will see many people who look like us. For the most part, they all have one head, two arms, two legs, and many are even dressed the same. They are all there for pretty much the same dream: They want to win! About the only thing that separates one person from another is our different personalities and the way we think. Anyway, from our vantage point above, we see most of these players losing their hard-earned money, all playing the same basic strategy. Now most of these people are just like you and me: fairly intelligent; with good, sound minds; and probably playing on a limited bankroll. However, they are all playing the same way, and for the most part, the majority of them are losing. Sure, there are a few winners, but not many. We have to assume that the only thing that separates the ones losing from the ones winning is a matter of luck or just sitting in the right chair at the right time.

My point is simply this: Basic strategy alone will not make you a consistent winner at the blackjack tables. All the books I have read on blackjack tell you that basic strategy is the way to play, based on the results of 10,000, 100,000, or millions of hands played on a high-speed computer. That's all well and good, but unless you are a professional player, it would take you years to play 100,000 hands of blackjack, let alone a million hands. In other words, basic strategy is based on the long run over a long period of time. Most of us don't think in terms of the long run because we have that basic human need of instant or immediate gratification. We want to win and we want the money right now, not over the long run. You are simply trying to win one hand and that's the one you're playing now. Besides, if most of these people are playing basic strategy and most of them are losing, it seems to make common sense that basic strategy does not work very well over a short period of time unless you can successfully count the cards (mentally keep a count of certain strategic cards played). We will talk more about card counting throughout this book, but I would like to stay on the subject of basic strategy just awhile.

Basic strategy was pretty much studied and designed in the 1960s. Folks, that was a long time ago! The only thing I know of that stays good that long is "true love." Regardless of this fact, basic strategy is still the most accepted way to play blackjack. However, in my opinion, things have changed. Casinos are no longer afraid of basic strategy players beating them, and, for that matter, they aren't that concerned about the counter either. Now take a minute to consider the following scenario and use your common sense.

Some individual, or a company, or a corporation decides to go into the gaming industry. They build a riverboat or a land-based casino, sometimes investing millions upon millions of dollars of their money. Finally, the casino is open and one of the games they offer for your enjoyment is blackjack. Now, these people are not stupid; they know there are many books out there that teach you how to play the game and the best way to beat it. These books teach you how to use basic strategy. But just in case you live in a cave or on a remote island and have never heard of basic strategy, the casinos themselves will give you or sell you for a dollar or two a little plastic chart of the basic strategy so that you can win the rest of the family jewels. Well, folks, this just doesn't make sense to me. Card counting coupled with basic strategy should, at least in theory, be unbeatable. However, I believe that countermeasures have been taken to protect those family jewels.

There are a lot of card-counting systems out there for you to learn and master. For the most part, these have been designed and devised by mathematicians and college professors—very intelligent people. I've read and tried most of them. Some, of course, are better than others; however, I consider myself an average-minded person. These card-counting systems are too damned hard to use. They wear you out mentally and fatigue you physically. I cannot count cards accurately. I can, however, tell when there is an excess of big cards played, or an excess of little cards played. I personally don't think that the majority of average players can count cards successfully; in my opinion, you would have to have a photographic memory to do so, and most of us certainly do not have this wonderful gift. Even if we did, we don't have X-ray vision to tell us what the next card off the deck will be; we only know that the chances are it will benefit our hand or break it, depending on the count. In other words, we have to have some idea of what the percentage is to make or break our hand by drawing one additional card.

Percentages are what the casinos base all their profits on—and they are huge profits. So it just makes sense to me to do the same thing—play the percentages.

It is my opinion that if we played every blackjack hand based on percentages only, we would have a much better chance to win money at the game. It doesn't matter if you are playing with one hand-held deck or eight decks out of a shoe. The percentage expectation of making or breaking your hand by drawing one additional card remains the same. The percentage expectation when the dealer has to draw (depending on the up card) remains the same also. Now, of course, once in a while you will run into a freaky shoe, where you will see six or seven face cards in a row, or six or seven little cards in a row, but the percentage will vary only 1 to 2 percent. If you can follow the cards and be observant, those freaky shoes shouldn't bother you. You can adjust your play accordingly.

There are several plays recommended by so-called experts and authors of books that I simply do not agree with. I don't think any gambling game can or should be played the same way every time. I believe it depends on the situation and the circumstances, and I will cover these and other plays later.

Please remember this: This book is not the Bible. There is nothing written in granite here. There will be times that you will vary your play and sometimes do exactly the opposite of what I have suggested here. That's okay too. Sometimes you just have to gamble to win. All I'm trying to do is eliminate some of that gamble from the game.

This book is written in terms the beginner can understand and the more advanced player has experienced. Its intention is to make you a successful blackjack player. You *can be,* but you must BELIEVE IT. My goal is to help you do just that.

This book is not about counting cards. It will not teach you to be a card counter. I can only hope that after reading it, you will have a new perspective on the game. There is always more than one way to look at anything; "percentage expectation" is just another way.

I mention several times in this book to listen to your intuition, your gut feeling, and to act on it. This book will add to your knowledge of the game of blackjack, and that will make you a smarter player. "Percentage expectation" will offer you a slightly different strategy to play by, with less to memorize, and you will be able to play with less mental stress.

I hope that after reading *Beat the Odds Blackjack,* you will be a "thinking" blackjack player. In other words, you will be a player that thinks and uses your mind before making decisions that affect your wallet—and the wallets of the other players. You can be a winner at this game. You are well on your way by reading this book.

BEAT THE ODDS
Blackjack

I

♥ ♣ ♦ ♠

Basic Beliefs and
Fallacies of the Game

I assume that all of us who have already been playing the game of blackjack have read at least one book on the subject, or were taught the basics of the game by another player who had previously read a book on it. I am also going to assume that you are not a card counter or you think counting cards is too hard for you to do.

When I first learned how to play blackjack, I was told always to assume the dealer's down card is a 10-count card. The next thing I was told was *never* to take insurance (see the Glossary) when the dealer had an Ace as an up card. I believed that and played that way for years until I realized that one statement contradicted the other. Sometimes it takes a while for the light to switch on. I'm not the sharpest knife in the drawer; I'm sure some of my critics will attest to that. Anyway, the facts are that the 10-count cards make up only *31* percent of the deck. This means the dealer's down card should be a 10-count card only *31* percent of the time. If we assume the down card is a 10-count card, we are assuming wrong *69* percent of the time.

Now, ladies and gentlemen, if we assume wrong *69* percent of the time, we are in deep yogurt financially. It is a cinch that we will go broke playing that way. DO NOT ASSUME THE DEALER'S DOWN CARD IS A 10-COUNT CARD!

Never taking insurance also is ridiculous. If you like your hand and want to play it or draw to it, by all means take insurance against the dealer's Ace. It all depends on your hand, and what you *think* the dealer has. Use your intuition. It is your friend and is usually right. You know this to be true. Use your intuition! Listen to it! Go with it! This will not be the last time you will see this word in this book. I will mention intuition many times. It is a powerful tool.

1

Splitting pairs will be covered in a separate chapter, but I want to mention here that it is nonsense to say that you always split Aces and 8s. Again, this depends on the dealer's up card and how the cards have been falling for you. If splitting them hasn't been working for you, DON'T KEEP DOING IT!

It is my purpose in writing this book to try to get you, as a blackjack player, to use your brain and common sense. Nothing, but nothing, should be an automatic course of action in this game. You are not playing in your kitchen for gum wrappers and toothpicks anymore. You are playing with money that you have probably worked hard for, so don't just give it away. THINK BEFORE YOU ACT ON YOUR HAND! It is also my intention to educate you on what your chances are with any given hand to improve it or break it. This book will not entertain you, but it will make you a better blackjack player and put money in your jeans pocket.

I'm sure, if you have played much blackjack in casinos, that you have heard the controversy about splitting face cards. This also will be covered in a later chapter (more than once). I see nothing wrong with it under the right conditions. Most of the people I see splitting face cards do it only when they have a pair of 10s, Jacks, Queens, or Kings. This leads me to believe they don't know that they can split any two-card combination of face cards. In other words, they don't have to be a pair; you can have a 10-Queen and split, or a Jack-King and split. Any two-card combo of 10-count cards can be split. The basic argument against it is that you are probably splitting up a winning hand and might end up with two losing hands. That, of course, is up to you. The game of blackjack is a gambling game and sometimes it pays off to gamble. Do whatever you want to, but know this up front. If you do split face cards, be prepared to see heads shaking, hear a lot of muttering, and maybe endure some name calling. You may even see grown men cry at the table. Especially if you split faces and the dealer makes a hand. You become the jackass at the table. But if you are at a full table and you have friends waiting to play, splitting face cards is a good way to get them a seat. I'm not going to tell you to split them or not to split them. In a later chapter I'm just going to let you know what to expect if you do. You're an adult; make your own decisions. This way, when you win, you can take all the credit, and when you lose, you will have nobody to blame but yourself. Remember, the only difference between a blackjack player and a new puppy is that eventually the puppy stops whining.

Several books I have read say that according to the computer, the average winning hand is 18½. Now folks, I have been playing blackjack for many, many years. Some of those years have been great winning years and some have not. I do not win every time I play and neither will you. But let me tell you this: In the hundreds of thousands of hands I've played, I have never, but never, looked down and found a hand of 18½. Never. Computer, my butt! I've also never seen a computer at a table playing blackjack. This is a game played by humans, being dealt to by another human. The basic strategy tables I have seen are based on the play of 100,000 hands or more. Do you have any idea how long it would take to play 100,000 hands of blackjack? Unless you are a professional player, which I doubt you are, you might play two days per week, if you live where there are casinos. You can play, on the average, about 50 hands per hour. If you play two days a week for, say, six hours each day, you will play 600 hands a week, or 2,400 hands a month. This comes to 28,800 hands per year. It would take you a little over three years and five months to play 100,000 hands. Also, you must understand that some basic strategy tables are based on the outcome of playing a million or more hands on a high-speed computer. This means that for you, a casual blackjack player, to achieve the same results the computer did, it would take over thirty-five years. Forget all that computer stuff. Use your own computer, your brain, and just try to win the hand you're playing right now. You may not play the identical hand the same way tomorrow.

In one very popular book on blackjack, according to the author's own chart of strategy, if you play the basic strategy the way he says to play it, you will, at the end of 100,000 hands, be a nine-hand loser. This is by his own chart. What's wrong with that picture?

2

♥ ♣ ♦ ♠

Card Counting—Does It Work?

One of the hardest things I have ever tried to accomplish is counting cards at a blackjack table in a busy casino. I can't do it! Too many distractions are coming at me from all directions. Exciting people, music, alcohol, a party atmosphere. I can't seem to hold my concentration and focus, and I lose count, getting frustrated and angry at myself for not being as brilliant as I think I am—or for that matter, even half as brilliant as I think I am.

To be a successful card counter, you must be as dedicated to it as a good doctor is to the medical profession. It takes hours each day to practice counting cards and you must be willing to sacrifice other things in your life to succeed at this art. For those of you who have become good card counters, I salute you. I am in awe of a mind that can be so focused.

For those of us who don't have that talent, however, or lack the commitment to learn how to count, we have to try other avenues to reach success. I believe "percentage expectation" is the right avenue for me—and I hope for you as well.

I'm not trying to start or get into any arguments over card counting, nor am I challenging anyone—and I'm not taking on any challenges; however, I simply don't think it works for many reasons. The majority of counters I know use a plus-minus counting system. In a six-deck game, that consists of 120 plus-count cards, the 2s, 3s, 4s, 5s, and 6s; 120 minus-count cards, the 10s, Jacks, Queens, Kings, and Aces; and 72 "zero-count" cards, the 7s, 8s, and 9s. Now this is where they lose me. We are told the 7s, 8s, and 9s are not important, yet we need these cards to make good hands out of the 12s, 13s, and 14s we constantly get. (Now, please no nasty cards or letters from those of you that are

4

proficient at this art. I truly admire your talents. I am aware that this is only one counting method and that there are others that count the Ace differently, and in some cases separately. However, for my purpose, this makes a good example.)

In counting cards, our success lies in being able to raise our bets when the deck becomes "rich" (in the player's favor), and to lower our bets when the deck becomes "lean" or "poor" (in the house's favor). The deck is said to be rich when there are more 10-count cards than there are non-10s, and lean when there are more non-10s than there are 10s. It is said that when there is an excess of 10s, it is to the player's advantage. Now to me, the dealer has the same chance of getting those 10-count cards as the player.

Anyway, when the deal begins, the count starts at zero. Every time a 10-count card or Ace shows up, you count it as a minus one, and when a 2, 3, 4, 5, or 6 shows, you count it as a plus one. You count each card as it shows up. Now, all of this makes logical sense to me if you go all the way through the six decks and use each card. Unfortunately, that's not the way it works. The dealer cuts off one to one and one-half decks that never come into play. That's 52 to 78 cards that never come into play. In reality then, when the deal starts and the card counter starts off with a count of zero, the actual count may be a plus five or six, or higher, or even a minus seven or eight or more, depending on the cards that have been cut off the back of the deck and out of play. We are to assume we have a "neutral" or an "even" mix of plus cards and minus cards back there. This is seldom the case. To check this out, simply get six decks of cards, take one and one-half decks—approximately 78 cards—out, and do the "plus"-"minus" thing and see what you have. The count will hardly ever be zero. For instance, if the out-of-play cards add up to a minus eight (eight more 10-count cards than non-10s) and you start your count at zero when play begins, then during the first part of the shoe your count goes to plus six, what happens? You start making larger bets based on your plus-six count when actually the count is minus two. Man! That will empty the pockets of every card counter on Bear Creek. You never can have an accurate count and your betting strategy is useless unless, of course, you just get lucky. On top of all this, if the pit boss thinks you are a card counter, he will instruct the dealer to cut off even more of the cards and reshuffle more often.

As far as I'm concerned, counting cards is good for just one thing: keeping your mind active and focused on the game. It forces you to

think and use your brain; it just simply is not accurate enough to consis-
tently win money for you. At least it isn't for me.

Card counting became the way to play in the 1960s, when Thorp
made the discovery, or at least made the discovery public, that blackjack
hands were not independent trials like the rolling of dice in a craps
game. In a craps game, each roll of the dice is an independent trial from
the preceding roll and of the next roll. One roll does not affect the
other. Not so in a blackjack game. In a blackjack game, the preceding
hand does affect the next hand because the cards played in the preceding hand are removed from the deck and placed out of the game. This
indeed affects the next hand and every hand thereafter. By keeping
track of the cards previously played and removed from the deck, you
could have some idea what your next hand might be. Card counting was
born! At that time blackjack was played with one deck (52 cards); they
were shuffled, cut by a player or the dealer, the top card was exposed
and turned face up on the bottom of the deck, and all the remaining
51 cards were used. When the face-up card appeared, the cards were
reshuffled and the game began again. It was easy to count cards then.
At least for some people it was.

Thorp also said this: "Las Vegas will come up with countermeasures
to offset the card counter." He made this statement more than once; in
fact, he made it so often, it sounded to me like a warning. He was right.
They began using multiple decks and cutting a large portion of cards
out of play, which nullified card counting. In addition to these things,
we now have to contend with playing with plastic cards and their self-
generating static electricity.

There's always been something about card counting that, truthfully,
I've never been able to understand. Back before all these books and
strategies on card counting came out, the casinos dealt the game of
blackjack with the player's cards face down. There was really no way to
keep an accurate card count by the average player with an average
mind. Then the books were published and a lot of publicity came out
about counting cards. The casinos were afraid of card counters and
began barring those players they suspected of being able to count. I
know a few players who were barred.

The thing that confuses me is if their systems were so great and card
counting was making the casinos tremble with fear, why did they start
dealing all the players' cards face up so that all cards were exposed and
so much easier to count and track? I have come to this conclusion: With

the dealer cutting one to one and one-half decks out of play, card counting is a waste of time and mental energy. At no time can you have an accurate count.

There you have the history of card counting and why I don't think it works. Think about it yourself. Let this explanation just lie around in your mind a few days and use your common sense, and I think you will agree with me on this one.

Does card counting work? In theory, certainly it does, but with all the obstacles the casinos have thrown up at us, in principle, I believe card counting is a money-losing proposition. I feel the same way about the so-called basic strategy we have been using for years—and losing our money by playing by it. In theory, sure it works, but it is based on the long haul, and most of us won't live long enough to see a profit using basic strategy. We need something for the short haul. Percentage expectation is that something.

3

Plastic Cards
(A Personal Pet Peeve)

Back in 1962, when Thorp wrote *Beat the Dealer,* the game of blackjack changed forever. It caused Las Vegas casinos to alter the rules of the game for a while and gave birth to the beginning of card counting. I was, and still am, very impressed with the author's mind and have made a lot of money from his pioneering of basic strategy. One thing he mentioned more than once was that Las Vegas would find a way to offset the card counters and basic strategy. I think they did just that. Keep in mind that I said this is what I *think.* I can't prove anything. The only thing I know is from personal experiences and thousands of hours in observing blackjack games. This is just a theory of mine.

When I began playing cards, we played with cards that were made of pressed paper. They were easy to shuffle, but they also bent easily. When plastic cards came into use, the casinos used them in their poker rooms only. I hated them right off the bat! You couldn't shuffle them as well. They were slippery and hard to hold on to. But there was something else about them. The flow of cards was different. Hands didn't make as often. The sequence was different. I know, I know, it sounds stupid. Plastic cards, when shuffled many times over a period of hours, create a kind of static electricity that causes the cards to cling or clump together. They don't separate. They seem to return to the same location in the deck. It's weird. Cards of a like kind seem to stick together; for instance, a face will follow a face, a 6 will follow a 6, etc. (Now, of course, I don't mean every time, but certainly enough that you need to be aware of this phenomenon.) All you have to do to check this out is to be observant at the tables.

When we would open a deck of pressed-paper cards, we would see they were arranged from the Ace to the deuce in all four suits. When plastic cards came into being, when we open a new deck, we find two suits arranged Ace to deuce and two suits arranged King to Ace. Why? Why did they make this seemingly small change in arrangement? Keep in mind this was done after the basic strategy came out.

My theory is this: When you open a new deck of plastic cards and begin to shuffle, you have basically two suits in your left hand arranged one way and two suits in your right hand arranged another. When you shuffle, you begin alternating one big card to one little card. With that combination and static electricity, those cards will stay in that order all day long. I know it sounds stupid, but I believe it. Ever wonder why you get so many 12 through 16 hands at a blackjack table? I mean more than normal. I see it all the time.

I know a card trick that's done with a new unshuffled deck. If you simply square cut the deck seven times and deal out seven five-card draw-poker hands, six players will have full houses and the dealer will have a straight flush. If a man can think up a card trick like that, there are men who can think of a way to shuffle a deck to benefit that eighth spot on a blackjack table.

Now, before we go any further, please understand that I am not saying the casinos or the dealers are cheating. I am saying the dealer's spot at the table is no different from any other spot, yet they seem to make hand after hand after hand. The dealers are no luckier than you are (yet at times you think they have ungodly luck!). So what does that leave us with as far as an explanation is concerned? It just leaves the cards and the house shuffle. A magician in California who specializes in card tricks told me of a shuffle that only a few magicians can do. Using a new deck and shuffling a set number of times, the deck will return to its original position. So if someone can think up that shuffle, how hard could it be to think up one that for the most part just alternates big cards with little cards? When you have alternating big cards and little cards, the card count never gets high enough for the card counter to benefit from it. Okay, I know what you are thinking because I can hear you laughing. This guy Cline is an idiot. Right? That's okay. It won't be the first time I've been called that. But you know what? I don't care. You cannot hurt my feelings on this one. I'm right and I know it. I can't prove anything and I have no scientific evidence to substantiate it, but over the last thirty-five years I have played more hands of poker and blackjack with these plastic-coated monsters than you will play in ten lifetimes and I know I'm right. This seems like a good place to tell a story about plastic cards and what I mean when I say "these same cards will continue coming to that spot."

I know this is a book about blackjack, but this incident took place in a poker game. The point, however, is the same. This is not an isolated case; I've seen similar situations many times over.

We were playing five-handed in an Omaha game, which is a "flop poker game." "Flop" poker is where there are five community cards "flopped" in the middle of the table. First the dealer flops three cards, then the fourth, then the fifth, to complete the board, with betting rounds in between. Five players are each shuffling at their own speed and rhythm, and each time, the deck is cut by a different player. The player to my right is the first dealer in this story, and he deals and "flops" the first three cards. I am needing a 10 for a straight, so I call the bet to see the fourth card. It is the 10 of spades, making my straight. It stands up and I win the hand. My deal, same game. Shuffle, deal, and "flop" the first three. I don't remember what they were, now I turn the fourth card up. It is the 10 of spades. Somebody wins. Next dealer, same game. Shuffle and deal, "flop" three, turn the fourth card. Guess what? The 10 of spades. Next dealer, same game. Do you want to guess what the fourth card is? You are right, the 10 of spades.

Point of story: Five different deals, five different dealers, five different styles of shuffling, and five times the 10 of spades is exactly in the same spot in the deck, the twenty-sixth card from the top.

What does this story have to do with blackjack? Nothing at all. Or does it? It has to do with plastic-coated cards and what I call plastic card sequence. All casinos use these plastic-coated cards and they definitely run in a pattern or sequence. Think I'm nuts? Do you ever notice how many times the dealer's first card is a face card and yours is a 4, 5, or 6? It wouldn't hurt you to be observant and once in a while ask yourself, "Why is that?" Okay, I got that off my chest. Sorry for the interruption, where was I? Oh yeah, stay focused on what you are doing and what you are seeing.

Let's get back to blackjack and how plastic cards affect the game. What happens is that you have players playing a systematic basic strategy all the same way and dealers using a systematic shuffle to offset it. What happens when you have systematic play against a systematic shuffle? Systematic results that are disastrous to the player and we walk away from the blackjack table scratching a broke ass. It doesn't have to be that way. If you aren't winning playing basic strategy, and you probably aren't unless you are playing heads-up (see the Glossary) with the dealer, try something different. Play the percentages as close as you can, but don't be afraid to gamble and hit more often until you make a hand of 15 or more. Do the unexpected.

Can you tell this subject of plastic cards really gets to me? Enough of this. The veins in my neck are pulsating. Let's get back to the subject of blackjack. Are you ready to play? Let's find a table (see Figure 1).

4

♥ ♣ ♦ ♠

Finding the Right Table

It is very important that you find the right table at which to play. After all, you may be planning a three- or four-hour playing session, and it's important that you build yourself a comfortable nest for that period of time.

Here are a few hints or ideas to look for in finding a table:

1. Select the right dealer. Personally, I prefer a female dealer over a male. She should be friendly, but not familiar. It's okay if she talks, but not constantly. I like a medium-paced game as far as speed is concerned, so I pay close attention to that. I refuse to play with a female dealer who moves to the rhythm of whatever music is being played, as if she were in a dance contest and not mentally involved in her job.

2. Choose a table that is not directly under a ventilation system. When it comes on, it becomes too hot or too cold for you to be comfortable.

3. Choose a table that is not directly in front of the "pit area's podium." There are too many distractions there.

4. If you like a specific spot at the table, make sure that spot is open and available.

5. Choose a "winning" table. Look at the players that are there. Are they smiling and have stacks of chips in front of them? If they are, it is a "winning" table. Are they talking to each other and having fun? If so, chances are it's a "winning" table.

6. Behind every blackjack table is the "dealer's tip box." You usually can't see it from the front of the table, but while standing in front of a row of tables, you can see the backs of the tables on the next row. Look at the "dealer's tip box." If it has a lot of chips in it, that table

has been "cold" all day and produced a lot of winners. Most players tip only when they are winning, so this is a very good sign that says loud and clear, "Hey, you, I am a cold dealer today." Get to that table as fast as you can.

Picking the right dealer and the right table is very important to you, so take your time doing it.

Getting Acquainted with the Blackjack Table

Some players have told me the blackjack table itself can be very intimidating. It is actually very "player friendly" and informative, as follows:

A. Discard rack.
B. Usually where the table sign is placed. This sign will state the rules of this table, including the minimum and the maximum limits.
C. The slot where your cash and the debit and credit slips are placed. There is a "cash drop" box directly under the slot.
D. The dealer's "chip" rack.
E. An electronic peeking device to determine the dealer's blackjack without him peeking at the hole card.

Figure 1. The Blackjack Table

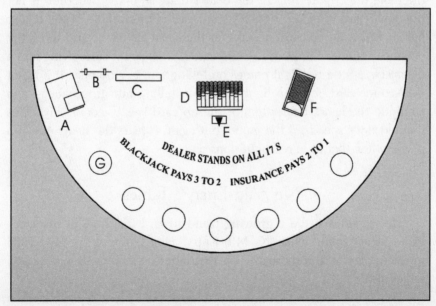

F. Dealing shoe; it holds four, six, or eight decks of cards.
G. Designates players' betting spaces. All bets are placed within the circles (sometimes squares).

No Fair Peeking!!!

In some casinos, and the number is getting larger every year, dealers are not allowed to "peek" at their down card when they have a 10-count card as an up card. After the players have all acted on their hands, the dealer then exposes his down card. Now, ladies and gentlemen, when that down card happens to be an Ace, giving the dealer a natural black-jack, you can just feel the air leave your body. In many cases, the players have made some great draws, maybe even some 21s, and for a few brief seconds they think they have won that hand or at least have a chance of winning it. Not so, and the players feel mentally demoralized. It has also wasted a lot of time playing the hand out when, if the down card had been known, the dealer would have simply announced his black-jack, collected the bets, and started another hand. This method is used to eliminate possible dealer-player collusion. In other words, it makes it impossible for the dealer to use any form of signaling to any player what his hole card might be because the dealer doesn't know what it is.

Fortunately, some casinos are installing electronic devices on top of the table directly in front of the dealer that can detect whether or not the down card is an Ace or a 10-count card. For example, if the dealer has an Ace as an up card, he asks for the usual insurance and slides the down card under the device. If the card is a 10-count card giving him a blackjack, a little red light comes on telling him to stop play; if it is not a 10-count card, a green light comes on telling him to go ahead and continue the hand. Same thing if the up card is a 10-count card. This method does speed up the game, but again it tears the heart out of a player when that little red light pops on.

"No Mid-Entry" Tables

There seems to be a growing trend toward this type of blackjack game. I have found most "No Mid-Entry" tables to be at the $10 to $25 minimum levels. But there are some casinos that employ this rule on $5 tables also.

This simply means that unless you are at the table and playing when the first hand is dealt, you cannot get in the game until the shoe or the deck is depleted and the cards have been reshuffled.

This type of play is used to discourage card counters from jumping into a game when the count is in the player's favor.

For the noncounter, it can work both to his advantage and to his disadvantage. It works to his advantage when the player is in a hot streak and making hands because another player cannot jump in and change the run of cards. Of course, the reverse is also true if the player is running cold and not making hands. In the latter case, hopefully the player would get up and move to another table.

Even if you are playing at a "No Mid-Entry" table and decide to play two hands, no can do! You must start with playing two hands in order to play two.

I like the concept of this rule and play at these tables when possible.

Surrender

Many of the casinos in my area offer an option to the game that I use from time to time to help in my money management (see page 60). It's one more decision the player has to make, and heaven knows we already have enough of those. However, this one comes in handy when you need it.

Surrender simply means, "I give up," "I throw in the towel," "Uncle." That's exactly what you do.

After receiving your original two cards and you decide you don't want to play them, you can "surrender" one-half of your bet and give your hand up.

Now, normally, being a "macho male," I don't like surrendering at anything. (Isn't that a ridiculous male thing?!?) However, many times this option has saved my bankroll, and I think you should be aware of it.

For instance, if you look down at your cards and see another 16 looking back at you and the dealer has a 10-count showing, you should consider surrendering. You will lose one-half of your bet, which is better than losing it all.

Surrendering is not something you want to get in the habit of doing every time you have a bad hand against a good up card, but when you think you are beat and you can save one-half of your bet, do it.

Personally, I surrender only when I have a 14, 15, or 16 and the dealer has a 10-count card as an up card. (By the way, you can't surrender when the dealer is showing an Ace.)

This is an excellent tool to add to your arsenal for money management. I just hope you don't get into the habit of surrendering all the time.

Be sure to read the sign on the table where you are playing to find out whether or not the casino offers it.

5

Blackjack Etiquette

In everything we do, there is usually a right and a wrong way to do it. This applies to playing blackjack as well. If you walk up to a table where there is only one player, playing the dealer heads-up, always ask that player if he would prefer playing alone or if you may join the table. Chances are he will invite you to sit down. If, however, he prefers playing alone, by all means let him.

Don't just walk up to a table and plop your butt and your bet down without checking out what the action is and whether or not the players are making hands or losing every bet. If they are on a hot streak and you jump in and change the run of things, they'll hate your guts. When the shoe is over, get in the next one. It's only polite not to barge in and it shows good manners. Be aware of the money players (players who bet $25 or more per hand). These players take the game very seriously. If you walk up to a table where there is a money player, try to take a position to his left and not to his right. This way he can't complain that you came in and took his good cards away.

When a new player comes to a table, the cards do change sequence, sometimes for the better and sometimes for the worse. Don't get me wrong here. You have every right to sit at any table you choose, at any time you choose. All I'm saying is, there is a right way and a wrong way. Good manners are always appropriate, whether you are at the blackjack table or the dinner table.

No one enjoys listening to a constant complainer or someone with a filthy mouth. Watch your language and treat your fellow players with kindness and respect, and they will probably treat you the same way.

Do not ever blame the dealer or another player for your losses. Nobody held a gun to your head and made you play, so accept the

17

responsibilities of your own actions. There will be times when this is extremely difficult to do. For example, when the player who is the last to act on his hand signals for a hit on his 14 when the dealer's up card is a 6 and he takes the break card away from the dealer, who, of course, draws a 4 to his 16 and makes a 20, which beats your 19, you will want to strangle the bastard for taking the dealer's break card. It happens, and you will experience it. Expect it. Remember this: Blackjack is not a team sport. The big winner at the table is not going to split his or her winnings with the other players. All you can do is play each hand by the percentages, and you will be able to do just that after reading this book. When the aforementioned incident happens, you can always resort to the power of prayer. The only difference between people who pray in church and people who pray in casinos is that the people who pray in casinos "really, really mean it." (Just kidding.) Believe me, if you act and talk the way you would if you were twelve years old and your mother was sitting next to you at the table, you will get along fine.

It is always good etiquette to tip when you are playing. I am sure that when you order a drink, you don't hesitate to tip the server. Most blackjack dealers are friendly, courteous, and seem sincere about wanting you to win. Their thinking is, of course, the more you win, the better chance they have of being tipped. I think the best way to tip a dealer is to place a bet for her when you are on a winning streak. You do this by placing a bet on the layout right in front of your bet. If you win your bet, the dealer pays off both your bet and the tip bet. A friend of mine has a good method of doing this. When he gets on a winning streak, he adds one extra dollar chip to his bet. After he wins that first bet, he puts the dollar chip out on the next hand for the dealer. He now has a dollar bet for the dealer and still has an extra dollar bet on his stack. This way, when he gets on a winning streak, the extra dollar bet on his hand becomes the tip bet on the next hand. He becomes a perpetual tipping machine and the casino is paying for it. The dealers love it and it creates good player-dealer relationships.

I think it is also important that you develop good blackjack etiquette with yourself. By this, I mean don't be so hard on yourself when you lose. You are not going to win every hand, and you're not going to win every time you play. You will have losing sessions. It's part of the game. Don't punish yourself mentally over the losses. It's bad for your self-esteem.

The language you use at the tables reflects who and what you are.

Don't be a jerk; you are in a public place and it shouldn't be necessary ever to use foul language. There is no excuse for it! Using that kind of language is a clear sign of the lack of self-control and the definite mark of a loser. It doesn't matter if you're male or female, it is in bad taste to use it and offensive to hear it.

A good rule to follow while playing is one you learned many years ago: Mind your own business! Not only is it good etiquette, it's just good common sense. It seems like there is a self-proclaimed expert at every table, ready and willing to advise everyone on how to play their hand. Don't let it be you. If someone wants your opinion on what is the correct way to play his hand, by all means share your knowledge with him, but just be sure you are a winner at the time. Giving your opinion when you are losing would be like me asking a friend of mine who's been married six times, what does it take to make a successful marriage?

Good etiquette is something always to keep in mind, regardless of what you are doing. If a person is ill-mannered and foul-mouthed at your table, it's a good idea just to find another table. It's not worth the discomfort and aggravation, or even embarrassment, to play there. Good manners are something someone either has or simply doesn't have. Well-behaved is something someone is or is not. I am sure no one has to remind you how to talk or behave in public.

6

Explanation of Percentages

Let me say here and now that ever since I started thinking and playing in terms of percentages, instead of trying to count cards or playing every hand according to basic strategy, my success rate has been much greater. I think yours will be too.

To my way of thinking, there really is no exact way to count cards or be totally accurate on percentages. That's mainly because of the fact that after the shuffle, the dealer cuts off that one to one and one-half decks that never come into play. That's 52 to 78 cards out of the shoe we cannot make a determination on. Therefore, any counting and any percentage will never be exact.

This is simply a guideline to educate you about your chances of making or breaking your hand. I am not going to clutter your mind with decimal points and fractions, but will simply reduce and round off to make the guideline as simple and easy to remember as I can. Keep in mind that it doesn't matter how many decks you use, the percentage stays the same. For my explanations, I will be basing all figures on a six-deck game, or 312 cards—96 10-count cards and 216 non-10s. That's 9 to 4 non-10s to 10s. For easier remembrance, just think 2 to 1 non-10s to 10s. The percentages I will be using will be by the hand and not by the shoe. I hope I'm not confusing you. It takes a variance of three cards to change the percentage 1 percent. Most hands will have an even distribution of non-10s to 10s, and with your mind and your eyes, you can observe if there is a big variance. If there is, you are a smart person and you can adjust the percentage. For the most part, it will remain the same.

There are 96 10-count cards in six decks, or 30.8 percent of the cards. There are 216 non-10s, or 69.2 percent of the cards.

For our purpose, I will round off to 31 percent 10-count cards and 69 percent non-10s. Just as an example, let's do this: If you have a stack of 312 cards and turn the top card face up on the table and it's a face card, what is the percentage that the next card will be a face card? The answer is that there is a 31 percent chance it will be a face card. If it is a face card, what is the percentage the next card will be a face card? Thirty-one percent. Now three face cards have been dealt and zero non-face cards. What is the percentage that the next card off will be a face card? The answer is now 30 percent. Got it?

On the following pages, I will take you step-by-step through what to expect when you have a stiff hand. The hands that you will get most often are the stiff hands. A "stiff" is any number that can be broken (exceed 21) by drawing one card to it. These stiff hands are 12 through 16. We will cover other hands such as 10 and 11 in the chapters on splitting pairs and doubling-down, but the stiff hands are the ones you will need to know how to play. These hands require your attention and concentration. They are the key to adding to or depleting your bankroll. You must learn how to play them or you will surely fail at playing this great game of blackjack. Please understand this fact. You are reading this book to learn and understand how to play this game, and this is the starting point.

7

Introduction to the Game

Let me begin by saying that the game of blackjack and the game of 21 are one and the same. It is not to be confused with the game of poker. With the recent widespread popularity of casino gambling, more people are being exposed to these games for the first time and there is some confusion. Many times I have asked, "Do you play poker?" and the answer is, "Yeah, I love it, but I don't get many blackjacks." Different games. Poker is poker. Blackjack is blackjack. This is a book on blackjack.

The object of blackjack is really very simple. As a matter of fact, the game itself is very simple to play, but make no mistake, it is not simple to win playing it. The object of blackjack is for you, as a player, *to beat the dealer!* You don't have to beat the other players at the table, and they don't have to beat you. Your hand has nothing to do with theirs, and theirs has nothing to do with yours. It is entirely your hand against the dealer's hand; whichever hand between yours and the dealer's is closest to the count of 21, without going over that count, is the "winner." To be the winner is the true object of blackjack. If you, the player, go over the count of 21 with your hand, you automatically lose that hand; you have "busted" your hand and have beaten yourself. I say, "You have beaten yourself," because you are the one who makes all the decisions concerning your hand. Whether or not to take additional cards is entirely up to you. It is my hope that after reading this book, you will make those decisions with knowledge and confidence.

The game of blackjack is played with one to seven players and one dealer. In most casinos in this country, a single-deck blackjack game is a thing of the past. Now the majority of blackjack games are played with four to eight decks. Since a six-deck game is the most prevalent where

22

I play, all figures, percentages, and numbers I'll be talking about in this book are based on playing blackjack with six decks dealt out of a card-holder called a "shoe." That is a game played with 312 cards. There are 96 10-count cards and 216 non-10 cards in a six-deck shoe. All the statements I make are based on a six-deck game, *but regardless of the number of decks used, the percentages remain the same.*

All the cards are counted with a number value. The 10s, Jacks, Queens, and Kings have a value of 10 and are all counted as 10. The Aces are counted as 1 or 11 and all other cards are counted at face value, e.g., 3 is counted as 3, a 7 is counted as 7, etc.

Before the dealer begins the deal, the player places his bet in the circle or square directly in front of him. Then play begins. The dealer deals from his left to his right, giving two cards, one each round, to each player at the table. The player's cards are dealt face up, and the dealer has one card face up (the up card) and one card face down (the hole card or down card). The dealer's up card is the foundation on which the players determine their strategy of play. For example, if the dealer's up card is a 7 through Ace, it is possible he does not have to draw any additional cards to his hand since the rules for the dealer are that he must hit a hand of 16 or less and stand with 17 or more. If his up card is a 2 through 6, then we know he is drawing at least one more card to his hand—and maybe more.

In most casinos today, the dealer must hit a soft 17. Example: A, 6 (Ace + 6) is a soft 17; so is A, 2, 4 (Ace + 2, 4) or A, 2, 2, 2 (Ace + 2, 2, 2). (See Figure 2.) We will discuss a soft hand in a later section. All figures and examples in this book are compiled from a blackjack game where the dealer must hit a soft 17. The table where you are playing will say right on the table layout, "The Dealer Must Hit Soft 17" or "The Dealer Stands on All 17s." Be sure to read the layout and all the signs on the table before you begin playing. These are the rules and the limits of this particular table and they change from table to table, sometimes even in the same casino. With this being the only rule for players, our common sense should tell us "don't go over the count of 21," which leads us back to stiff hands and why it is so very important to know how to play them.

The only rule for the player is simply this: "If you go over the count of 21, you lose." The rules for the dealer are also simple and very rigid. The dealer must hit 16 and stand on 17. There is, however, this variation of the rule. Some casinos stand on soft 17 while some hit on soft 17. It

Figure 2

Here are three examples of a "soft"-count hand. A soft hand is simply a hand that cannot be broken (exceed 21) by drawing just one card. All three of these hands total 7, or "soft" 17. As you can see, if the player decides to draw an additional card here and draws a 10-count card, he would then have a "hard" 17.

A "soft" hand is easy to count, but for some reason confuses some players. Count the hand on the left as 1 + 6 = 7 plus 10 left over from the Ace = 17; you have 7, or a "soft" 17. The middle hand is 1 + 2 = 3 + 4 = 7 + 10 left over from the Ace = 17; you have 7, or a "soft" 17. The hand on the far right is 1 + 2 = 3 + 2 = 5 + 2 = 7 and 10 left over from the Ace = 17; you have 7, or a "soft" 17.

is important to you, as a player, to know how the casino you are in plays a soft 17. Read the layout on the table.

Anyway, back to the beginning of play. After the dealer has shuffled the cards and offered them to be cut by a player, the cards are loaded into a "shoe." The dealer removes one card from the shoe and places it face down in the discard rack. This is the "burn" card. The dealer then begins the deal: two rounds of cards face up to the players and one card up and one card down to himself. Beginning at the dealer's left, the first player makes a hand signal to indicate whether or not he needs or wants any additional cards. When it is your turn to signal that you want another card or "hit," you scratch the table surface with your fingers in a motion toward yourself; to signal no cards or "stand," you put your hand out flat, palm down, and move it back and forth horizontally over your cards. After all players have acted on their hands, the dealer turns his hole card up, announces the total, then either draws additional cards or stands, depending on the total count. Again, the dealer must hit 16 and stand on 17.

If any player has a "blackjack," which is an original two-card combination of an Ace and any 10-count card, he is paid at a payoff of 3 to 2. If a player and the dealer both have a blackjack, it is a "push" or a tie and the player keeps his bet. Anytime a player and the dealer have the same total count, it is a push, unless the player has a count of 21 and the dealer turns over a two-card natural blackjack. A two-card natural blackjack beats all other hands that total 21 (see Figure 3).

For the dealer to have a blackjack, he must have a 10-count card up and an Ace as his down card, or an Ace up and a 10-count card down. If the 10-count card is the up card, the dealer will check for a blackjack. If he has an Ace in the hole, he turns it over, declares he has a blackjack, and collects your money. However, if he has an Ace as his up card, he

Figure 3

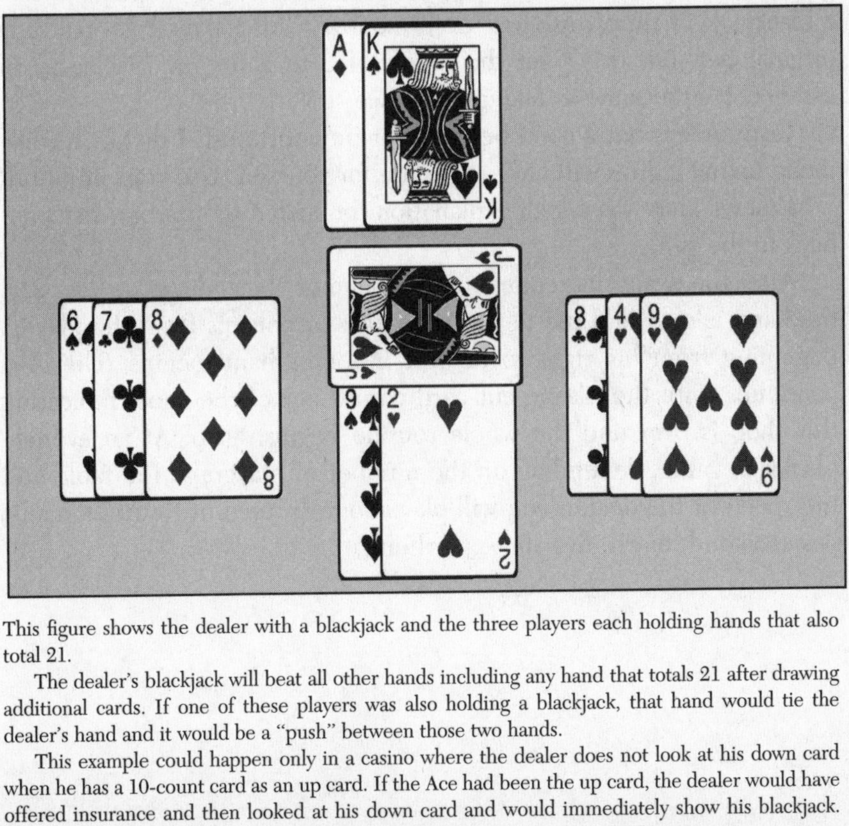

This figure shows the dealer with a blackjack and the three players each holding hands that also total 21.

The dealer's blackjack will beat all other hands including any hand that totals 21 after drawing additional cards. If one of these players was also holding a blackjack, that hand would tie the dealer's hand and it would be a "push" between those two hands.

This example could happen only in a casino where the dealer does not look at his down card when he has a 10-count card as an up card. If the Ace had been the up card, the dealer would have offered insurance and then looked at his down card and would immediately show his blackjack.

will ask the players if they want "insurance." As you can see on the table layout (see page 13), insurance pays 2 to 1 on your bet. Insurance bets seem to confuse some players, but it's a pretty simple part of the game.

Insurance is a separate bet from your original one. It really has nothing to do with it. You are simply saying "I think he has a blackjack" when you take insurance, or "I don't think he has a blackjack" when you don't take insurance.

You can bet up to one-half of your original bet if you take insurance. In other words, if your bet is $10 and the dealer turns up an Ace, you can bet up to $5 that he has a blackjack. Let's say you take insurance and bet the $5. The dealer does not have a blackjack and he takes your $5 and you play your hand to a conclusion. However, if he would have had a blackjack, you would have lost your $10 original bet, but you would have been paid 2 to 1 on your $5 insurance bet, so you would get your $10 bet returned to you. Whether or not you take insurance is entirely up to you. I personally don't take insurance unless I have a blackjack myself. When that happens (dealer has an Ace up and I have a blackjack), I simply ask for "even money." This means I get paid my original bet, but don't get the bonus of 3 to 2 for my blackjack. In essence, it's the same as taking insurance.

Insurance is not a good bet, and for the most part, I do not recommend taking it. You will have to decide for yourself. Use your intuition.

Whew! That was a long explanation for such a simple bet. Let's get back to the game.

After the dealer has completed his hand or "busted" (gone over 21), the hand is over and the dealer then pays or collects from the players beginning from his right to his left. Another hand begins. The deal continues until the plastic cut card comes out of the shoe, indicating this shoe is over and the whole routine begins again. At an average blackjack game, depending on the number of players at the table and the speed of the dealer, you will play about thirteen or fourteen hands per shoe and four to five shoes per hour.

8

♥ ♣ ♦ ♠

The Basis of Percentage Playing

In figuring what my chances are or what the percentage is on breaking or improving my hand by taking an additional card, I use the following procedure.

It will help you to store the following information in your long-term memory if you use the art of visualization. Picture, if you will, in your mind's eye six decks of cards, already shuffled and stacked in one stack of 312 cards. (You can try this at home with just one deck if you want; the percentages will still be the same.)

Now take the top card and turn it face up. It doesn't matter what the card is, but let's say it is a 5. Now take the next card off the top of the stack without looking at it. Place it under the first card face down. Now you have a dealer's hand.

Since the up card is a 5, we know for sure the dealer has to draw at least one card to complete or break the hand. What are the chances this hand is a good hand to draw to? In other words, what are the chances the dealer is drawing to a total of 7, 8, 9, 10, or 11? To find out, just add up the 2s, 3s, 4s, 5s, and 6s. There are 120 cards minus the 5 that is the up card for a total of 119 cards, or 39 percent of the cards. The dealer has a 39 percent chance of drawing to a good hand of 7, 8, 9, 10, or 11. He has a 7 percent chance of drawing to a total of 6, and a 54 percent chance of drawing to a breaking hand. Now with that kind of information we can make an intelligent decision on how to play our hand.

Please keep in mind these percentages are approximate, but within 1 to 2 percent of being accurate. There will be some freaky shoes where you will experience some "clumping" of the cards. Clumping is when there is an abnormal number of 10-count cards all bunched together, or an abnormal number of non-10 cards bunched up. This is pretty common with plastic cards because of the static electricity they generate. When the shoe is running normal, there should be a 10-count card about every third card. It might be easier for you to remember the percentages this way. If the dealer's up card is 2 through 6, his chance of drawing to a good hand of 7, 8, 9, 10, or 11 is the same 39 percent. The dealer has only a 31 percent chance of having a 10-count card in the hole. That's why I say, if you have been told to assume the dealer's hole card is a 10-count card, you are assuming wrong 69 percent of the time. If you are wrong 69 percent of the time, you will lose! Period! If the dealer's up card is 7 through 10, there is a 39 percent chance he is drawing to a breaking hand of 12 through 16 (a hand that may "break" or go over 21 when the dealer hits) and a 39 to 61 percent chance of being pat (not drawing), depending on what the up card is.

What to Expect When the Dealer's Up Card Is a 2 Through 6

Here are some guidelines to follow when trying to decide what to do with your hand when the dealer's up card is a:

2
- There is a 39 percent chance he is drawing to a 7, 8, 9, 10, or 11.
- There is only a 31 percent chance he is drawing to a breaking hand (i.e., 12 through 16).
- There is a 30 percent chance he is drawing to a number less than 7.

3
- There is a 39 percent chance he is drawing to a 7, 8, 9, 10, or 11.
- There is a 39 percent chance he is drawing to a breaking hand.
- There is a 22 percent chance he is drawing to a number less than 7.

4
- There is a 39 percent chance he is drawing to a 7, 8, 9, 10, or 11.
- There is a 46 percent chance he is drawing to a breaking hand.
- There is a 15 percent chance he is drawing to a number less than 7.

5
- There is a 39 percent chance he is drawing to a 7, 8, 9, 10, or 11.
- There is a 53 percent chance he is drawing to a breaking hand.
- There is an 8 percent chance he is drawing to a number less than 7.

6

- There is a 39 percent chance he is drawing to a 7, 8, 9, 10, or 11.
- There is a 61 percent chance he is drawing to a breaking hand.

But always keep this in mind: Unless the dealer is standing on a soft 17, anytime the up card is 2 through 6, there is a 100 percent certainty that he does have to draw. Anytime the dealer has to draw, the better it is for the player.

As you can see, anytime the dealer's up card is a 2 through 6, there is a 39 percent chance he is drawing to a good hand, and a 61 percent chance he is drawing to a bad hand. In other words, when the dealer has a 6 up ten times, he should be drawing to a good hand of 7, 8, 9, 10, or 11 four times, and drawing to a breaking hand six times.

What to Expect When the Dealer's Up Card Is a 7 Through an Ace

The following is a guideline to follow when trying to decide what to do with your hand when the dealer's up card is a:

7

- There is a 22 percent chance he is drawing to a 9, 10, or 11.
- There is a 39 percent chance he is drawing to a breaking hand.
- There is a 39 percent chance he is pat.

8

- There is a 15 percent chance he is drawing to a 10 or 11.
- There is a 39 percent chance he is drawing to a breaking hand.
- There is a 46 percent chance he is pat.

9

- There is a 7 percent chance he is drawing to an 11.
- There is a 39 percent chance he is drawing to a breaking hand.
- There is a 54 percent chance he is pat.

10 (Any Face Card)

- There is a 39 percent chance he is drawing to a breaking hand.
- There is a 61 percent chance he is pat.

Let's take a second to pause and talk about the 10-count up card here. You will see a lot of them. So many, in fact, you will want to puke. Remember earlier we mentioned assuming a 10-count as a down card? Look at the percentage. For every ten times he has a 10-count up, he is drawing to a breaking hand four of those times. My point here is simply this: Don't be intimidated by the 10-count card.

Ace

- There is a 31 percent chance he has a blackjack.
- There is a 23 percent chance he is pat.
- There is a 46 percent chance he is drawing.

Interesting figures here. If the dealer does not have a blackjack, it is 2 to 1 he has to draw. We will talk about this situation several times in this book.

Now you can see we have the same percentages if the dealer's up card is 7 through 10 as when it is a 2 through 6. Only now they are reversed. There is a 39 percent chance he is drawing to a breaking hand, and a 61 percent chance he is pat or drawing to a good hand.

When the dealer is showing an Ace, there is only a 31 percent chance that he has a blackjack. If you get past that possibility, the percentage that he is drawing is in your favor. Any time the dealer has to hit his hand and draw, the player has the advantage.

What to Expect from the Dealer's Hand Regardless of the Up Card

The dealer's spot on the table is no different from the first-base or the third-base spot, or your spot on the table. They are all the same. I know at times it doesn't seem like it, but they are.

Out of every 100 hands, the dealer will have 36 to 42 pat hands (see the Glossary), depending on whether he is running hot or cold, and will have to draw at least one card 58 to 64 hands. In a lot of these 58 to 64 hands, he will have a 10-count card as an up card. Do not be intimidated by that 10-count card and do not continue to hit your hand until you've busted your hand and your bankroll. *Let the dealer break!*

To see for yourself how percentage expectation works, try this at home. Using a standard deck of 52 cards, shuffle and turn the top card face up. Let's say it is a face card. This is the dealer's up card. Now count off the next ten cards. Three or four of these cards will produce a draw to a breaking hand of 12, 13, 14, 15, or 16 (for 39 percent), and six or seven of these cards will produce a pat hand of 17, 18, 19, 20, or 21 (for 61 percent). Do it again. This time the up card is a 5. Count off the next ten cards. Three to four of these cards will produce a draw to a good hand of 7, 8, 9, 10, or 11 (for 39 percent), and five to six cards will produce a draw to a breaking hand of 12, 13, 14, 15, or 16 (for 54 percent); zero to one card will produce a draw to the number 6 (for 7 percent). Percentage expectation is that simple.

What to Do with Your Hand When the Dealer's Up Card Is a 2 Through 6

I assume you know to hit your hand if you are holding a total of 9 or less. If you did not know that, you do now. We are speaking here of the problem hands, or the stiff hands, 12 through 16.

- If you are holding a 12, hit except when the dealer is showing a 4, 5, 6, or Ace. I suggest you seldom hit a breaking hand against a 4, 5, 6, or Ace (see Chapter 27, The Player's Strategy Guide, p. 94).
- If you are holding a 13, hit except when the dealer is showing a 3, 4, 5, 6, or Ace (see the Player's Guide).
- If you are holding a 14, hit except when the dealer is showing a 2, 3, 4, 5, 6, or Ace (see the Player's Guide).
- If you are holding a 15 or 16, you are in trouble and you can expect to lose these hands. If you hit, you are going against the percentages, so I suggest you stand on these hands and hope the dealer is drawing and breaks his hand. The dealer will break 32 to 36 percent of the time if you will just give him a chance to do so. You will get a lot of these hands because there are 288 possible two-card combinations that will make a 14, 15, or 16. If you are at a table where you are getting a lot of 14s, 15s, or 16s, get up and move. You don't have any Velcro on your butt, so go to another table. With plastic cards, these same hands will continue coming to that spot. Move!! I know it is frustrating when this happens, but if you just sit there, you will get angry and lose control. When that happens, no book or system will help you. Stay focused on what you are doing.

What to Do with Your Hand
When the Dealer's Up Card Is a 7 Through an Ace

If you are holding a stiff hand (12 through 16) and the dealer is showing a possible pat hand, these are the guidelines to follow:

- If you are holding a 12, hit until you have 15 or more.
- If you are holding a 13, hit until you have 15 or more.
- If you are holding a 14, hit until you have 15 or more.
- If you are holding a 15 or 16, again, I suggest you stand pat and take your chances that the dealer will break his hand.

Do not be intimated just because the dealer has a big card showing. With six decks being used, there are a lot more mice than there are elephants in the deck. I know what you're thinking now: "If that's true, why wouldn't I hit when I have 15 or 16?" The answer is simple: When the player breaks his hand, the player loses. Even if the dealer breaks, the player has already lost his money. The percentages are too big against you to hit 15 or 16. Let the dealer break instead of you.

9

♥ ♣ ♦ ♠

How Percentage Expectation Works

If you as a player are holding a 12, the following is what can happen to the hand if you hit it:

1. You can catch an Ace, giving you a 13, which means you have a 39 percent chance of breaking on your next card, and a 39 percent chance of making a 17, 18, 19, 20, or 21. Your chances are even that you will make a good hand or you will break.
2. You can catch a deuce, giving you a 14, which means you have a 46 percent chance of breaking on your next card, and a 39 percent chance of making a 17, 18, 19, 20, or 21. The chances are better that you will break than they are of making a good hand.
3. You can catch a 3, giving you a 15, which means you have a 54 percent chance of breaking on your next card, and a 39 percent chance of making a 17, 18, 19, 20, or 21. Same thing here. Chances are you will break if you hit.
4. You can catch a 4, giving you a 16, which means you have a 61 percent chance of breaking on your next card, and a 39 percent chance of making a 17, 18, 19, 20, or 21.
5. You can catch a 5, giving you a 17, which means you have a 69 percent chance of breaking on your next card, and a 31 percent chance of making an 18, 19, 20, or 21.
6. You can catch a 6, giving you an 18, which means you have a 76 percent chance of breaking on your next card, and a 24 percent chance of making a 19, 20, or 21.
7. You can catch a 7, giving you a 19, which means you have an 84 percent chance of breaking on your next card, and a 16 percent chance of making a 20 or 21.

8. You can catch an 8 giving you a 20, which means you have a 93 percent chance of breaking on your next card, and a 7 percent chance of making a 21.
9. You can catch a 9 giving you a 21, which means you have a 100 percent chance of breaking on your next card. (I know you're not going to hit a 21, are you?)
10. You can catch a 10 and break your hand with a 22, and there is a 31 percent chance you will.

With any hand of 12 through 16, you have a 39 percent chance of improving it to a 17, 18, 19, 20, or 21, and your chances of breaking increase from 31 percent with a 12 to 61 percent with a 16.

Comments on "Stiff" Hands

When the player is holding a stiff hand of 12 through 16 (see Figure 4), the player should know that the percentage expectation of making a good hand of 17, 18, 19, 20, or 21 is always a constant 39 percent, no matter which of those five numbers he is holding.

It is *only the percentage expectation for breaking the hand* that increases with the higher total number. In other words, there is no difference between holding a 12 and holding a 16 as far as your chances are of making a good hand, but a big difference in your chances of breaking the hand.

That's why the player must learn some discipline and patience and not hit as often, giving the dealer a chance to break his hand. Remember this: As long as the player hasn't busted out his hand, he always has a chance of winning, but once he breaks his hand, the fat lady has sung.

Player's Stiff Totals Played Against Dealer's Up Cards

When a player holds a 12, he has a 31 percent chance of breaking. When he holds a 13, he has a 39 percent chance of breaking. When he holds a 14, he has a 46 percent chance of breaking. When he holds a 15, he has a 54 percent chance of breaking. When he holds a 16, he has a 61 percent chance of breaking.

When the dealer's up card is a 2 through 6, he has a 31 to 61 percent chance that he is drawing to a breaking hand, depending on whether

Figure 4

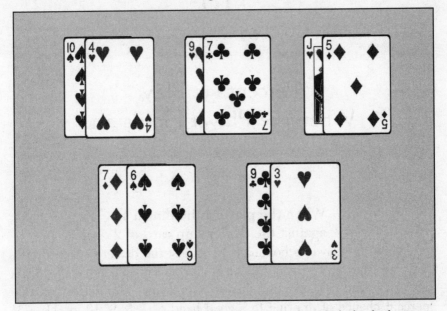

A stiff hand is any hand that totals 12 through 16. All of these hands can be broken by drawing an additional card. The 12 can be broken by drawing a 10-count card; the 13 by drawing a 9 or 10-count; the 14 by drawing an 8, 9, or 10-count; the 15 by drawing a 7, 8, 9, or 10-count; and the 16 by drawing a 6, 7, 8, 9, or 10-count.

You will get these hands more often than any other hands, and you must learn to play them correctly if you want to be successful at this game. If you find you are getting more than your share of these stiff hands, don't get angry or frustrated—get up and move to another table.

the up card is a 2, 3, 4, 5, or 6. Regardless of what card—2 through 6—is the up card, however, there is a constant 39 percent chance the dealer is drawing to a good hand of 7, 8, 9, 10, or 11.

When the dealer's up card is 7 through 10, there is a 39 percent chance he is drawing to a breaking hand, and a 39 to 61 percent chance he is pat, depending on whether the up card is a 7, 8, 9, or 10.

IO

Percentage Play:
When the Player Holds a 12

When the player is holding a 12
against the dealer's up card of 2

When the player is holding a 12 against the dealer's up card of 2, the player has a 39 percent chance of making a good hand of 17, 18, 19, 20, or 21, and a 31 percent chance of breaking. The dealer has a 39 percent chance of drawing to a good hand of 7, 8, 9, 10, or 11; a 31 percent chance of drawing to a breaking hand of 12; and a 30 percent chance of drawing to a number less than 7. The player has a better chance of making a hand than he does of breaking. The dealer seems to always make a hand with a deuce as an up card. Hit your 12 against the dealer's up card of 2. Hit!

When the dealer's up card is 3

When the player is holding a 12 against the dealer's up card of 3, the player has a 39 percent chance of making a good hand of 17, 18, 19, 20 or 21, and a 31 percent chance of breaking. The dealer has a 39 percent chance that he is drawing to a hand of 7, 8, 9, 10, or 11; a 39 percent chance he is drawing to a breaking hand of 12 or 13; and a 22 percent chance he is drawing to a number less than 7. The player has a better chance of making a hand than breaking, and the dealer's chances are even. Hit your 12 against the dealer's up card of 3. Hit!

When the dealer's up card is a 4

When the player is holding a 12 against the dealer's up card of 4, the player has a 39 percent chance of making a good hand of 17, 18, 19, 20, or 21, and a 31 percent chance of breaking. The dealer has a 39 percent chance that he is drawing to a good hand of 7, 8, 9, 10, or 11; a

46 percent chance he is drawing to a breaking hand of 12, 13, or 14; and a 15 percent chance he is drawing to a number less than 7. The player has a better chance of making a hand than he does of breaking, but that big 46 percent chance that the dealer has of drawing to a breaking hand is not worth the player drawing. Stand on your 12 against the dealer's up card of 4. Stand!

When the dealer's up card is a 5

When the player is holding a 12 against the dealer's up card of 5, the player has a 39 percent chance of making a good hand of 17, 18, 19, 20, or 21, and a 31 percent chance of breaking. The dealer has a 39 percent chance of drawing to a 7, 8, 9, 10, or 11; a 54 percent chance of drawing to a breaking hand of 12, 13, 14, or 15; and a 7 percent chance of drawing to a number less than 7. The player has a better chance of making a hand than he does of breaking, but that huge 54 percent chance that the dealer has of drawing to a breaking hand should stop you from even thinking about it. Stand on your 12 against the dealer's up card of 5. Stand!

When the dealer's up card is a 6

When the player is holding a 12 against the dealer's up card of 6, the player has a 39 percent chance of making a good hand of 17, 18, 19, 20, or 21, and a 31 percent chance of breaking. The dealer has a 39 percent chance of drawing to a 7, 8, 9, 10, or 11, and a whopping 61 percent chance of drawing to a breaking hand of 12, 13, 14, 15, or 16. (I am assuming that the dealer draws to a soft 17.) The player has a better chance of making a hand than he does of breaking, but with that whopping 61 percent chance the dealer has of drawing to a breaking hand, any player should be hung with a wet rope if he even thinks about hitting in this situation. Stand on your 12 against the dealer's up card of 6. Stand!

When the dealer's up card is a 7

When the player is holding a 12 against the dealer's up card of 7, the player has a 39 percent chance of making a good hand of 17, 18, 19, 20, or 21, and a 31 percent chance of breaking. The dealer has a 22 percent chance of drawing to a good hand of 9, 10, or 11; a 39 percent chance of drawing to a breaking hand of 12, 13, 14, 15, or 16; and a 39 percent chance of being pat. The player has a better chance of making a hand than he does of breaking, and with the dealer's chances of 61 percent that he is drawing to a good hand or is pat, the player should hit his 12 against the dealer's up card of 7. Hit!

When the dealer's up card is an 8

When the player is holding a 12 against the dealer's up card of 8, the player has a 39 percent chance of making a good hand of 17, 18, 19, 20, or 21, and a 31 percent chance of breaking. The dealer has a 15 percent chance of drawing to a 10 or 11; a 39 percent chance of drawing to a breaking hand of 12, 13, 14, 15, or 16; and a 46 percent chance of being pat. The player has a better chance of making a hand than he does of breaking, and with the dealer's chances of 61 percent that he is drawing to a good hand or is pat, the player should hit his 12 against the dealer's up card of 8. Hit!

When the dealer's up card is a 9

When the player is holding a 12 against the dealer's up card of 9, the player has a 39 percent chance of making a good hand of 17, 18, 19, 20, or 21, and a 31 percent chance of breaking. The dealer has a 7 percent chance of drawing to an 11; a 39 percent chance of drawing to a breaking hand of 12, 13, 14, 15, or 16; and a 54 percent chance of being pat. The player has a better chance of making a hand than he does of breaking, and with the dealer's chances of 61 percent that he is drawing to a good hand or is pat, the player should hit his 12 against the dealer's up card of 9. Hit!

When the dealer's up card is a 10

When the player is holding a 12 against the dealer's up card of 10, the player has a 39 percent chance of making a good hand of 17, 18, 19, 20, or 21, and a 31 percent chance of breaking. The dealer has a 39 percent chance of drawing to a breaking hand, and a 61 percent chance of being pat. The player has a better chance of making a hand than he does of breaking, and with the dealer's 61 percent chance of being pat, the player should hit his 12 against the dealer's up card of 10. Hit!

When the dealer's up card is an Ace

When the player is holding a 12 against the dealer's up card of an Ace, the player has a 39 percent chance of making a good hand of 17, 18, 19, 20, or 21, and a 31 percent chance of breaking. The dealer has a 31 percent chance of having a blackjack, a 46 percent chance of having to draw, and a 23 percent chance of being pat. The player has a better chance of making a hand than he does of breaking; however, if the dealer does not have a blackjack, it's 2 to 1 he will have to draw. It is my opinion that the player should stand against the dealer's up card of an Ace. (Assuming the dealer is hitting a soft 17.) Stand!

If you are playing in a casino where the dealer stands on a soft 17, hit your 12 against the Ace up card! (This is an extremely controversial call, and this writer, and this book, will receive some criticism over this one, but I believe I am right.)

Summary

When the player is holding a 12 against any up card except a 4, 5, 6, or Ace, he should hit and try to make a hand of 15 or more. As you can see, I do not recommend hitting any stiff hand against an up card of 4, 5, 6, or Ace. A lot of people will argue about standing on 12 against an Ace, but as I said, if the player can escape the dealer having a blackjack, it is 2 to 1 odds the dealer has to draw. It is my opinion that anytime the dealer has to draw, the better it is for the player. Always remember that the biggest advantage the house has over the player is that the player has to act on his hand first.

Playing a stiff hand (12–16) all the time is no fun and it is not very profitable. If it seems to you that you are getting more than your share, I suggest you move to another table. As I've said before, you're not strapped in your chair, so just move.

However, you can expect to make a lot of stiff hands just based on percentages. There are 420 ways to make a two-card combination of hands 12–16, and only 276 ways to make a two-card pat hand of 17–21. That means that 33 percent of the time you can expect to have 12–16, but only 21 percent of the time will you have a pat hand of 17–21.

As you may have noticed, the player's chances of making a good hand of 17–21 while holding a starting hand of 12–16 are all the same: 39 percent, as are the dealer's chances of drawing to a good hand while showing an up card of 2–6, the same 39 percent. The dealer's chances then reverse themselves when showing an up card of 7–10, with him having a 39 percent chance of drawing to a breaking hand of 12–16. It is also interesting to note that all the stiff hands that a player can hold

have the same 39 percent chance of making a good hand, and only the
chance for breaking increases as the total increases.

There are 108 possible ways to make a two-card 12, not counting
the combination of A, A, for obvious reasons. The dealer will get his
share too, so don't feel bad when you get yours.

II

♥ ♣ ♦ ♠

Percentage Play: When the Player Holds a 13

When the player is holding a 13 against the dealer's up card of 2

When the player is holding a 13 against the dealer's up card of 2, the player has a 39 percent chance of making a hand of 17, 18, 19, 20, or 21, and a 39 percent chance of breaking. The dealer has a 39 percent chance of drawing to a good hand of 7, 8, 9, 10, or 11; a 31 percent chance of drawing to a breaking hand of 12; and a 30 percent chance of drawing to a number less than 7. The player has an even chance of making or breaking his hand, while the dealer has a better chance of making a hand than he does of breaking. Hitting a 13 against a dealer's up card of 2 is a close call, but I like to be aggressive in this situation. Hit your 13 against the dealer's up card of 2. Hit!

When the dealer's up card is a 3

When the player is holding a 13 against the dealer's up card of 3, the player has a 39 percent chance of making a hand of 17, 18, 19, 20, or 21, and a 39 percent chance of breaking. The dealer has a 39 percent chance of drawing to a good hand of 7, 8, 9, 10, or 11; a 39 percent chance of drawing to a breaking hand of 12 or 13; and a 22 percent chance of drawing to a number less than 7. Both player and dealer have good chances of making or breaking their hand, but with the dealer's 22 percent chance of drawing to a number less than 7, let the dealer draw. Stand on your 13 against the dealer's 3. Stand!

When the dealer's up card is a 4

When the player is holding a 13 against the dealer's up card of 4, the player has a 39 percent chance of making a hand of 17, 18, 19, 20,

41

or 21, and a 39 percent chance of breaking. The dealer has a 39 percent chance of drawing to a good hand of 7, 8, 9, 10, or 11; a 46 percent chance of drawing to a breaking hand of 12, 13, or 14; and a 15 percent chance of drawing to a number less than 7. The player has an even chance of making or breaking his hand, while the dealer has a better chance of breaking his hand than he does of making it. Stand on your 13 against the dealer's 4. Stand!

When the dealer's up card is a 5

When the player is holding a 13 against the dealer's up card of 5, the player has a 39 percent chance of making a good hand of 17, 18, 19, 20, or 21, and a 39 percent chance of breaking. The dealer has a 39 percent chance of drawing to a good hand of 7, 8, 9, 10, or 11; a 54 percent chance of drawing to a breaking hand of 12, 13, 14, or 15; and a 7 percent chance of drawing to a number less than 7. The player has an even chance of making or breaking his hand, while the dealer has a big 54 percent chance he is drawing to a breaking hand. Let the dealer draw to his hand. Stand on your 13 against the dealer's 5. Stand!

When the dealer's up card is a 6

When the player is holding a 13 against the dealer's up card of 6, the player has a 39 percent chance of making a good hand of 17, 18, 19, 20, or 21, and a 39 percent chance of breaking. The dealer has a 39 percent chance of drawing to a good hand of 7, 8, 9, 10, or 11, and a whopping 61 percent chance of drawing to a breaking hand of 12, 13, 14, 15, or 16. The player has an even chance of making or breaking his hand, while the dealer has that big 61 percent chance he is drawing to a breaking hand. Let the dealer break. Stand on your 13 against the dealer's 6. Stand!

When the dealer's up card is a 7

When the player is holding a 13 against the dealer's up card of 7, the player has a 39 percent chance of making a good hand of 17, 18, 19, 20, or 21, and a 39 percent chance of breaking. The dealer has a 22 percent chance of drawing to a 9, 10, or 11; a 39 percent chance of being pat; and a 39 percent chance of drawing to a breaking hand of 12, 13, 14, 15, or 16. The player has an even chance of making or breaking his hand, while the dealer has the 23 percent chance of drawing to a good hand plus the 39 percent chance of being pat. Hit your 13 against the dealer's up card of 7. Hit!

When the dealer's up card is an 8

When the player is holding a 13 against the dealer's up card of 8, the player has a 39 percent chance of making a good hand of 17, 18, 19, 20, or 21, and a 39 percent chance of breaking. The dealer has a 15 percent chance he is drawing to a 10 or 11; a 46 percent chance he is pat; and a 39 percent chance he is drawing to a breaking hand of 12, 13, 14, 15, or 16. The player has an even chance of making or breaking his hand, while the dealer has the 15 percent chance of drawing to a 10 or 11 plus the 46 percent chance he is pat. Hit your 13 against the dealer's up card of 8. Hit!

When the dealer's up card is a 9

When the player is holding a 13 against the dealer's up card of 9, the player has a 39 percent chance of making a good hand of 17, 18, 19, 20, or 21, and a 39 percent chance of breaking. The dealer has a 7 percent chance of drawing to an 11; a 54 percent chance of being pat; and a 39 percent chance of drawing to a breaking hand of 12, 13, 14, 15, or 16. The player has an even chance of making or breaking his hand, while the dealer has the 7 percent chance of drawing to an 11 plus that big 54 percent chance of being pat. Hit your 13 against the dealer's up card of 9. Hit!

When the dealer's up card is a 10

When the player is holding a 13 against the dealer's up card of 10, the player has a 39 percent chance of making a good hand of 17, 18, 19, 20, or 21, and a 39 percent chance of breaking. The dealer has a 39 percent chance of drawing to a breaking hand, and a whopping 61 percent chance of being pat. The player has an even chance of making or breaking his hand, while the dealer has that big 61 percent chance of being pat. Hit your 13 against the dealer's up card of 10. Hit!

When the dealer's up card is an Ace

When the player is holding a 13 against the dealer's up card of an Ace, the player has a 39 percent chance of making a good hand of 17, 18, 19, 20, or 21, and a 39 percent chance of breaking. The dealer has a 31 percent chance of having a blackjack, a 23 percent chance of being pat, and a 46 percent chance that he is drawing. The player has an even chance of making or breaking his hand. If the player can escape the 31 percent chance of the dealer having a blackjack, it is 2 to 1 the dealer has to draw. Let the dealer draw to his hand. Stand on your 13 against the dealer's up card of an Ace. Stand!

It's the same situation here that we have when holding a 12 against an Ace. If the dealer is hitting a soft 17, you stand on your 13 against the Ace. If the dealer is standing on a soft 17, you hit your 13 against the Ace up card! (I know, more controversy, but I still believe I am right.)

Summary

When the player is holding a stiff hand of 13, he has a 39 percent chance of making a good hand of 17–21, and the same chances of breaking. If you are an aggressive player, you may choose to hit more often than I have suggested here. I know that some of you will disagree with me on standing on a 13 against an Ace. That's okay. Remember: There's nothing written in granite here. This book is written to educate you on your chances of making or breaking your hand and the chances the dealer has of doing the same thing. My opinion comes from years of playing and observing the game, and I am just sharing that information with you. Playing a stiff hand is a big part of blackjack and you must learn to play it in a confident way. Don't forget to listen to your intuition. There are 120 possible ways to make a two-card 13, counting the A, 2 for a soft 13. More ways than any other two-card total. Don't get discouraged when you get your share. Expect them and know how to play them.

Percentage Play:
When the Player Holds a 14

When the player is holding a 14 against the dealer's up card of 2

When the player is holding a 14 against the dealer's up card of 2, the player has a 39 percent chance of making a good hand of 17, 18, 19, 20, or 21, and a 46 percent chance of breaking. The dealer has a 39 percent chance of drawing to a good hand of 7, 8, 9, 10, or 11; a 31 percent chance of drawing to a breaking hand of 12; and a 30 percent chance of drawing to a number less than 7. The player has a better chance of breaking than he does of making a hand. The dealer has a 31 percent chance of drawing to a breaking hand plus the 30 percent chance of drawing to a number less than 7. Let the dealer draw. Stand on your 14 against the dealer's up card of 2. Stand!

When the dealer's up card is a 3

When the player is holding a 14 against the dealer's up card of 3, the player has a 39 percent chance of making a good hand of 17, 18, 19, 20, or 21, and a 46 percent chance of breaking. The dealer has a 39 percent chance of drawing to a good hand of 7, 8, 9, 10, or 11; a 39 percent chance of drawing to a breaking hand of 12 or 13; and a 22 percent chance of drawing to a number less than 7. The player has a better chance of breaking than he does of making his hand. The dealer has a 39 percent chance of drawing to a breaking hand plus the 22 percent chance of drawing to a number less than 7. Let the dealer draw to his hand. Stand on your 14 against the dealer's up card of 3. Stand!

When the dealer's up card is a 4

When the player is holding a 14 against the dealer's up card of 4, the player has a 39 percent chance of making a good hand of 17, 18, 19,

20, or 21, and a 46 percent chance of breaking. The dealer has a 39 percent chance of drawing to a good hand of 7, 8, 9, 10, or 11; a 46 percent chance of drawing to a breaking hand of 12, 13, or 14; and a 15 percent chance of drawing to a number less than 7. The player has a better chance of breaking than he does of making a hand. The dealer has a 46 percent chance of drawing to a breaking hand plus the 15 percent chance of drawing to a number less than 7. Let the dealer draw. Stand on your 14 against the dealer's 4. Stand!

When the dealer's up card is a 5

When the player is holding a 14 against the dealer's up card of 5, the player has a 39 percent chance of making a good hand of 17, 18, 19, 20, or 21, and a 46 percent chance of breaking. The dealer has a 39 percent chance of drawing to a good hand of 7, 8, 9, 10, or 11; a 54 percent chance of drawing to a breaking hand of 12, 13, 14, or 15; and a 7 percent chance of drawing to a number less than 7. The player has a better chance of breaking than he does of making a hand. The dealer has a big 54 percent chance of drawing to a breaking hand plus the 7 percent chance of drawing to a number less than 7. Let the dealer draw. Stand on your 14 against the dealer's up card of 5. Stand!

When the dealer's up card is a 6

When the player is holding a 14 against the dealer's up card of 6, the player has a 39 percent chance of making a good hand of 17, 18, 19, 20, or 21, and a 46 percent chance of breaking. The dealer has a 39 percent chance of drawing to a good hand of 7, 8, 9, 10, or 11, and a whopping 61 percent chance of drawing to a breaking hand of 12, 13, 14, 15, or 16. The player has a better chance of breaking than he does of making a hand. The dealer has that big 61 percent chance of drawing to a breaking hand. By all means, let the dealer draw. Stand on your 14 against the dealer's 6. Stand!

When the dealer's up card is a 7

When the player is holding a 14 against the dealer's up card of 7, the player has a 39 percent chance of making a good hand of 17, 18, 19, 20, or 21, and a 46 percent chance of breaking. The dealer has a 22 percent chance of drawing to a 9, 10, or 11; a 39 percent chance of being pat; and a 39 percent chance of drawing to a breaking hand of 12, 13, 14, 15, or 16. The player is in a hard spot here. He has a 46 percent chance of breaking, but the dealer has a total of a 61 percent chance of drawing to a 9, 10, or 11, or being pat. I think you have to gamble here to have a shot at winning. Hit your 14 against the dealer's up card of 7. Hit!

When the dealer's up card is an 8

When the player is holding a 14 against the dealer's up card of 8, the player has a 39 percent chance of making a good hand of 17, 18, 19, 20, or 21, and a 46 percent chance of breaking. The dealer has a 15 percent chance of drawing to a good hand of 10 or 11; a 46 percent chance of being pat; and a 39 percent chance he is drawing to a breaking hand of 12, 13, 14, 15, or 16. The player has a better chance of breaking than he has of making a hand. Again, he is between a rock and a hard place. The dealer has a total of a 61 percent chance he is drawing to a 10 or 11, or he is pat. Hit your 14 against the dealer's up card of 8 and try to get lucky. Hit!

When the dealer's up card is a 9

When the player is holding a 14 against the dealer's up card of 9, the player has a 39 percent chance of making a good hand of 17, 18, 19, 20, or 21, and a 46 percent chance of breaking. The dealer has a 7 percent chance of drawing to an 11, a 54 percent chance of being pat, and a 39 percent chance of drawing to a breaking hand of 12, 13, 14, 15, or 16. The player has a better chance of breaking than he does of making a hand. The dealer has a total of a 61 percent chance he is drawing to an 11 or he is pat. Again, you have to try to make a hand. Hit your 14 against the dealer's up card of 9. Hit!

When the dealer's up card is a 10

When the player is holding a 14 against the dealer's up card of 10, the player has a 39 percent chance of making a good hand of 17, 18, 19, 20, or 21, and a 46 percent chance of breaking. The dealer has a 61 percent chance of being pat, and only a 39 percent chance of drawing to a breaking hand of 12, 13, 14, 15, or 16. The player has a better chance of breaking than he does of making a hand. With the dealer having a 61 percent chance of being pat, hit your 14 against the dealer's up card of 10. Hit!

When the dealer's up card is an Ace

When the player is holding a 14 against the dealer's up card of an Ace, the player has a 39 percent chance of making a good hand of 17, 18, 19, 20, or 21, and a 46 percent chance of breaking. The dealer has a 31 percent chance of having a blackjack, a 23 percent chance of being pat, and a 46 percent chance that he is drawing. The player has a better chance of breaking than he does of making a hand. If the dealer does not have a blackjack, it is 2 to 1 he has to draw. Let the dealer draw. Stand on your 14 against the dealer's up card of an Ace. Stand!

Summary

When a player is holding 14, again he is stuck between a rock and a hard place. With a 46 percent chance of breaking, I don't think it is worth the risk to hit it, except when the dealer is showing an up card of 7–10. Same argument here about standing against the dealer's Ace. It is extremely hard for a player to stand on a bad hand against an Ace, but since I have forced myself to do it, I am winning more hands and that's what it is all about. Don't let yourself be intimidated by the dealer's up card of an Ace.

There are 108 possible ways to make a two-card 14, counting the A, 3 for a soft 14, so know in advance you will be getting them, but so will the dealer.

13

♥♣♦♠

Percentage Play: When the Player Holds a 15

When the player is holding a 15 against the dealer's up card of 2

When the player is holding a 15 against the dealer's up card of 2, the player has a 39 percent chance of making a hand of 17, 18, 19, 20, or 21, and a 54 percent chance of breaking. The dealer has a 39 percent chance of drawing to a good hand of 7, 8, 9, 10, or 11; a 31 percent chance of drawing to a breaking hand of 12; and a 30 percent chance of drawing to a number less than 7. The player has a better chance of breaking than he does of making a hand. The dealer has a 31 percent chance of drawing to a breaking hand plus the 30 percent chance of drawing to a number less than 7. Let the dealer draw. Stand on your 15 against the dealer's up card of 2. Stand!

When the dealer's up card is a 3

When the player is holding a 15 against the dealer's up card of 3, the player has a 39 percent chance of making a hand of 17, 18, 19, 20, or 21, and a 54 percent chance of breaking. The dealer has a 39 percent chance of drawing to a good hand of 7, 8, 9, 10, or 11; a 39 percent chance of drawing to a breaking hand of 12 or 13; and a 22 percent chance of drawing to a number less than 7. Again, the player has a better chance of breaking than he does of making a hand. The dealer has a 39 percent chance of drawing to a breaking hand of 12 or 13 plus the 22 percent chance of drawing to a number less than 7. Let the dealer draw. Stand on your 15 against the dealer's up card of 3. Stand!

When the dealer's up card is a 4

When the player is holding a 15 against the dealer's up card of 4, the player has a 39 percent chance of making a good hand of 17, 18, 19,

49

20, or 21, and a 54 percent chance of breaking. The dealer has a 39 percent chance of drawing to a good hand of 7, 8, 9, 10, or 11; a 46 percent chance of drawing to a breaking hand of 12, 13, or 14; and a 15 percent chance of drawing to a number less than 7. The player has a better chance of breaking than he does of making a hand. The dealer has a 46 percent chance of drawing to a breaking hand of 12, 13, or 14 plus the 15 percent chance of drawing to a number less than 7. Let the dealer draw. Stand on your 15 against the dealer's 4. Stand!

When the dealer's up card is a 5

When the player is holding a 15 against the dealer's up card of 5, the player has a 39 percent chance of making a good hand of 17, 18, 19, 20, or 21, and a 54 percent chance of breaking. The dealer has a 39 percent chance of drawing to a good hand of 7, 8, 9, 10, or 11; a 54 percent chance of drawing to a breaking hand of 12, 13, 14, or 15; and a 7 percent chance of drawing to a number less than 7. Again, the player has a better chance of breaking than he does of making a hand. The dealer has a 61 percent chance he is drawing to a breaking hand of 12, 13, 14, or 15, or to a number less than 7. Let 'im draw. Stand on your 15 against the dealer's up card of 5. Stand!

When the dealer's up card is a 6

When the player is holding a 15 against the dealer's up card of 6, the player has a 39 percent chance of making a good hand of 17, 18, 19, 20, or 21, and a 54 percent chance of breaking. The dealer has a 39 percent chance of drawing to a good hand of 7, 8, 9, 10, or 11, and a 61 percent chance of drawing to a breaking hand of 12, 13, 14, 15, or 16. The player has a better chance of breaking than he does of making a hand. The dealer has a big 61 percent chance of drawing to a breaking hand so let the dealer draw. Stand on your 15 against the dealer's 6. Stand!

When the dealer's up card is a 7

When the player is holding a 15 against the dealer's up card of 7, the player has a 39 percent chance of making a good hand of 17, 18, 19, 20, or 21, and a 54 percent chance of breaking. The dealer has a 22 percent chance of drawing to a good hand of 9, 10, or 11; a 39 percent chance of being pat; and a 39 percent chance of drawing to a breaking hand of 12, 13, 14, 15, or 16. This is a much closer call than it looks like.

I say let the dealer draw. Stand on your 15 against the dealer's up card of 7. Stand!

When the dealer's up card is an 8

When the player is holding a 15 against the dealer's up card of 8, the player has a 39 percent chance of making a good hand of 17, 18, 19, 20, or 21, and a 54 percent chance of breaking. The dealer has a 15 percent chance of drawing to a good hand of 10 or 11; a 46 percent chance of being pat; and a 39 percent chance of drawing to a breaking hand of 12, 13, 14, 15, or 16. The player has a better chance of breaking than he does of making a hand. I get a lot of arguments here, but I don't mind arguing. Give the dealer a chance to break. Stand on your 15 against the dealer's up card of 8. Stand!

When the dealer's up card is a 9

When the player is holding a 15 against the dealer's up card of 9, the player has a 39 percent chance of making a good hand of 17, 18, 19, 20, or 21, and a 54 percent chance of breaking. The dealer has a 7 percent chance of drawing to an 11; a 54 percent chance of being pat; and a 39 percent chance of drawing to a breaking hand of 12, 13, 14, 15, or 16. The player has a better chance of breaking than he does of making a hand. Here we go again. Let the dealer break. Stand on your 15 against the dealer's up card of 9. Stand!

When the dealer's up card is a 10

When the player is holding a 15 against a dealer's up card of 10, the player has a 39 percent chance of making a good hand of 17, 18, 19, 20, or 21, and a 54 percent chance of breaking. The dealer has a 61 percent chance of being pat, and a 39 percent chance of drawing to a breaking hand of 12, 13, 14, 15, or 16. The player has a better chance of breaking than he does of making a hand. The dealer has a 61 percent chance of having a pat hand. Damned if you do, damned if you don't. I'm sticking to my guns here. Stand on your 15 against the dealer's up card of 10. Stand!

When the dealer's up card is an Ace

When the player is holding a 15 against the dealer's up card of an Ace, the player has a 39 percent chance of making a good hand of 17, 18, 19, 20, or 21, and a 54 percent chance of breaking. The dealer has a 31 percent chance of having a blackjack, a 23 percent chance of being pat, and a 46 percent chance that he is drawing. The player has a better chance of breaking than he does of making a hand. If the dealer does not have a blackjack, it is 2 to 1 he will be drawing. Let him draw. Stand on your 15 against the dealer's up card of an Ace. Stand!

Summary

A 15 is one of the toughest hands to play in blackjack. With a 54 percent chance of breaking, if you don't hit, there is no way to win unless the dealer breaks his hand. I know it doesn't seem like it, but the dealer gets these stiff hands just as often as the player does. The problem is, when the dealer's up card is a 7 or higher, we automatically put him on a pat hand and that's a huge mistake. The dealer will break 36 percent of the time if the players will only give him a chance to hit. You don't have to have a good hand to win in this game. A lot of money has been won on stiff hands by just being patient and letting the dealer break. There are 96 possible ways to make a two-card 15, counting the A, 4 for a soft 15, so expect to see a lot of them.

14

♥ ♣ ♦ ♠

Percentage Play: When the Player Holds a 16

When the player is holding a 16 against the dealer's up card of a 2

When the player is holding a 16 against the dealer's up card of 2, the player has a 39 percent chance of making a hand of 17, 18, 19, 20, or 21, and a 61 percent chance of breaking. The dealer has a 39 percent chance of drawing to a good hand of 7, 8, 9, 10, or 11; a 31 percent chance of drawing to a breaking hand of 12; and a 30 percent chance of drawing to a number less than 7. When the player has a 61 percent chance of breaking, it's best to let the dealer draw to his hand. Stand on your 16 against the dealer's up card of 2. Stand!

When the dealer's up card is a 3

When the player is holding a 16 against the dealer's up card of 3, the player has a 39 percent chance of making a hand of 17, 18, 19, 20, or 21, and a 61 percent chance of breaking. The dealer has a 39 percent chance of drawing to a good hand of 7, 8, 9, 10, or 11; a 39 percent chance of drawing to a breaking hand of 12 or 13; and a 22 percent chance of drawing to a number less than 7. When the player has a 61 percent chance of breaking, it's best to let the dealer draw to his hand. Stand on your 16 against the dealer's up card of 3. Stand!

When the dealer's up card is a 4

When the player is holding a 16 against the dealer's up card of 4, the player has a 39 percent chance of making a good hand of 17, 18, 19, 20, or 21, and a 61 percent chance of breaking. The dealer has a 39 percent chance of drawing to a good hand of 7, 8, 9, 10, or 11; a 46 percent chance of drawing to a breaking hand of 12, 13, or 14; and a 15

53

percent chance of drawing to a number less than 7. When the player has a 61 percent chance of breaking, it's best to let the dealer draw to his hand. Stand on your 16 against the dealer's up card of 4. Stand!

When the dealer's up card is a 5

When the player is holding a 16 against the dealer's up card of 5, the player has a 39 percent chance of making a good hand of 17, 18, 19, 20, or 21, and a 61 percent chance of breaking. The dealer has a 39 percent chance of drawing to a good hand of 7, 8, 9, 10, or 11; a 54 percent chance of drawing to a breaking hand of 12, 13, 14 or 15; and a 7 percent chance of drawing to a number less than 7. When the player has a 61 percent chance of breaking, it's best to let the dealer draw. Stand on your 16 against the dealer's up card of 5. Stand!

When the dealer's up card is a 6

When the player is holding a 16 against the dealer's up card of 6, the player has a 39 percent chance of making a good hand of 17, 18, 19, 20, or 21, and a 61 percent chance of breaking. The dealer has a 39 percent chance of drawing to a good hand of 7, 8, 9, 10, or 11, and a 61 percent chance of drawing to a breaking hand of 12, 13, 14, 15, or 16. By all means, let the dealer draw to his hand. Stand on your 16 against the dealer's up card of 6. Stand!

When the dealer's up card is a 7

When the player is holding a 16 against the dealer's up card of 7, the player has a 39 percent chance of making a good hand of 17, 18, 19, 20, or 21, and a 61 percent chance of breaking. The dealer has a 22 percent chance of drawing to a good hand of 9, 10, or 11; a 39 percent chance of being pat; and a 39 percent chance of drawing to a breaking hand of 12, 13, 14, 15, or 16. When the player has a 61 percent chance of breaking, it's best to just hope the dealer has to draw. Stand on your 16 against the dealer's up card of 7. Stand!

When the dealer's up card is an 8

When the player is holding a 16 against the dealer's up card of 8, the player has a 39 percent chance of making a good hand of 17, 18, 19, 20, or 21, and a 61 percent chance of breaking. The dealer has a 15 percent chance of drawing to a good hand of 10 or 11; a 46 percent chance of being pat; and a 39 percent chance of drawing to a breaking hand of 12, 13, 14, 15, or 16. The player is still up against that brick wall of a 61 percent chance of breaking. Again, hold your breath and hope the dealer has to draw. Stand on your 16 against the dealer's up card of 8. Stand!

When the dealer's up card is a 9

When the player is holding a 16 against the dealer's up card of 9, the player has a 39 percent chance of making a good hand of 17, 18, 19, 20, or 21, and a 61 percent chance of breaking. The dealer has a 7 percent chance of drawing to an 11; a 54 percent chance of being pat; and a 39 percent chance of drawing to a breaking hand of 12, 13, 14, 15, or 16. I'm sure you know the routine by now—the player's chances of breaking are too big for taking a card. Stand on your 16 against the dealer's up card of 9. Stand!

When the dealer's up card is a 10

When the player is holding a 16 against a dealer's up card of 10, the player has a 39 percent chance of making a good hand of 17, 18, 19, 20, or 21, and a 61 percent chance of breaking. The dealer has a 61 percent chance of being pat, and a 39 percent chance of drawing to a breaking hand of 12, 13, 14, 15, or 16. Same old story—say a prayer and keep your fingers crossed. Stand on your 16 against the dealer's up card of 10. I know, I know, but stand on it anyway. Stand!

When the dealer's up card is an Ace

When the player is holding a 16 against the dealer's up card of an Ace, the player has a 39 percent chance of making a good hand of 17, 18, 19, 20, or 21, and guess what? A 61 percent chance of breaking. The dealer has a 31 percent chance of having a blackjack, a 23 percent chance of being pat, and a 46 percent chance of drawing. If the player escapes the dealer having a blackjack, it is 2 to 1 the dealer has to draw. Stand on your 16 against the dealer's up card of an Ace. Stand!

Summary

Sixteen! Every blackjack player's nightmare hand. There are 84 ways to make a two-card 16, counting A, 5 as a soft 16, so don't be surprised when it seems like you're getting more than your share. The dealer gets them too. Just make sure you're still in the game when he does. With that big 61 percent chance of breaking, you should never hit a 16 against any card the dealer might be showing.

15

♥ ♣ ♦ ♠

The Mother-in-Law Hand

When the dealer is holding a hand of 17, he must stand on it. That's the rule! Hit on 16 or less, and stand on 17 or more (with the exception, of course, of hitting a soft 17).

The player doesn't have any such rule. When a player is holding a hand of 17, chances are he is not going to hit it. However, the only way you can win on a 17 is if the dealer breaks. If the dealer makes a hand, the best you can hope for is a push.

This is what will or could happen if you wanted to hit your 17: You could catch an Ace, 2, 3, or 4 and improve your hand, but you have only a 31 percent chance of doing that and a 69 percent chance of breaking. I am certainly not going to advise you to hit a 17, although I do from time to time. If you are making a lot of 17s and not winning on them, hit one once in a while. This will, if nothing else, change the run of the cards. You might even get lucky and make a miracle draw *and* change the run of the cards and your luck.

Seventeen is called the mother-in-law hand because sometimes you want to hit it, but if you do, chances are you'll get into trouble.

16

♥♣♦♠

The Bankroll

Before we get into splitting pairs and doubling-down, let's take a break from the boring and tedious reading of statistical data and talk about two very important facets of this game: the bankroll and money management.

To play and enjoy this great game of blackjack, every player needs a bankroll. To keep playing and enjoying the game requires that you know how to protect that bankroll.

Just what is a bankroll? A bankroll is the amount of money you take with you to the casino with which to gamble. As a matter of fact, the size or dollar amount of your bankroll should determine what minimum-limit blackjack game you choose to play in. The bankroll can be any size you can afford it to be. It is not the rent money, or the grocery money, or the car payment money. It should be money that is used for only one thing, and that one thing is to gamble; in this case, to play blackjack with. If you do not know how to protect it, you will soon be out of the blackjack-playing business. It is never wise to risk your entire bankroll during a single playing session.

As a young boy, I played baseball after school with the other boys in the neighborhood. First, we had to find a boy that had a baseball. After we found a ball, we would go to the vacant lot down the street, or just in the street itself, and choose sides and start playing. We might play for hours or for just a few minutes, depending on just one thing: whether or not we lost the ball. Your bankroll is the ball for this game of black-jack, and how long you get to play depends on whether or not you lose it.

It's important that you know and realize that with a small bankroll you must play at a smaller-limit table. I like to use the guideline of 30

57

bets minimum to stay within my bankroll. If I have a bankroll of $100, I must limit myself to playing at a $3 minimum table. If I have $150 bankroll, I can safely play at a $5 table; and with a $300 bankroll, I would feel comfortable at a $10 minimum table. You can do the math to find out how big a bankroll is necessary for a $25 table, or a $100 table, but chances are that since you are reading this book, you are a $3 to $10 player—and that's fine. Don't ever let yourself think that you are inferior in any way, or that you don't belong at that blackjack table, just because you don't have as much money as the next player.

From this point on, I will be referring to a $300 bankroll and playing at a $10 minimum table. And usually at a $10 minimum table you have a $1,000 maximum, although some casinos have a $500 maximum on $10 minimum tables. Just read the little sign that is on the table to know the minimum and the maximum bets.

Let me wander off the subject of the bankroll for just a minute and do a little explaining and assuming. Since there are so many states that now have legalized casino gambling (thirty-three was the last count I had), and since you bought and are reading this book to learn how to play blackjack, I am assuming that you are planning on playing quite often (at least a couple of times per week) and are not just a once-a-year player. To my way of thinking, the frequency of your play has a lot to do with how you play and manage your bankroll. In other words, if you and the Mrs. (or Mr.) are flying off to Vegas for a few days for some fun and frolic, you aren't too interested in how to manage your bankroll. On the other hand, if you live where there are casinos right down the street and are planning on playing in them quite often, then you need to know this information and it is written and directed to this kind of player.

Okay, here we go again. You've got your $300 bankroll in your pocket and are entering the casino. At this point, you should have already decided on how much money you are going to try to win. Ten or twenty thousand dollars is a nice round number, but totally unrealistic to use as a goal. You need to have a "win" goal in mind—a realistic "win" goal. It is important that you know how to win and that you develop a habit of winning. By learning the playing strategy in this book, you will know "how" to win, and by setting realistic "win" goals, you will be able to develop a "habit" of winning.

A realistic "win" goal for a $300 bankroll is 30 percent, or $90. Sounds pretty simple, doesn't it? I mean, you're at a $10 table and if you bet all minimum bets of $10, all you have to do is win nine hands more than you lose to reach your win goal of $90. Simple, right? Wrong! While playing blackjack is easy to do, winning at blackjack is not as easy. It is like taking candy from a grizzly bear! There are many variables to contend with, like a bad run of cards, losing a double-down or a split, crowded conditions at the table, distracting casino noises, human errors, forgetting the strategy, etc., etc.

Your $300 bankroll is on the endangered species list. What may happen here is very common. I see it every day at virtually every table. While you have a good playing strategy and a decent bankroll for the limit you are playing for, there is still something missing. And that something is money management or bankroll management. A bankroll and money management go hand in hand; you can't have one without needing the other.

17

♥ ♣ ♦ ♠

Money Management

Good bankroll management requires patience, self-control, and a betting system or method that you, as a player, believe in and have confidence using.

I am going to give you three different betting methods, tell you not to use one of them, and then let you pick which of the other two you would prefer using with your style of play.

One of the oldest methods of betting is the "double-up method," or the Martingale system. With this system, the thinking is very logical, but for other reasons it is doomed to failure. The idea here is you start with a single unit bet (in our case, we are at a $10 minimum table with a $300 bankroll); so we bet our $10 and lose. Now the system requires we double-up our bet and bet $20. We lose this bet also. Now we bet $40. I'm sure you can see where this is headed. The idea behind this system is simply that we will eventually win a bet and receive a profit of $10. This is "stinkin' thinkin'," for two very good reasons: The first reason should be obvious to us, and that is the fact that the dealer can get on a "hot streak" or we can get on a "cold streak." It is not uncommon for the player to lose several hands in a row. It is unfortunate, but not uncommon. Simple math tells us that after only four losing bets and betting the fifth hand, we have exceeded our bankroll. But even if we were to pull out more money, after losing the sixth bet in a row, we have to bet $640 and in some cases that exceeds the table limit and the bet cannot be made. DO NOT EVEN THINK ABOUT USING THIS SYSTEM OF BETTING!

This next system of betting is called the 2-1-2 system and is for the conservative player. Since our bankroll is only $300, we need to play conservatively and this system will help protect our bankroll. This system is based on the theory that most shoes will run "choppy." In other words, the player will win a hand, then the dealer will win a hand; back and forth; back and forth. This system has a built-in "regression" bet that I like, which gives us a chance to show a plus in the win column, even if we are going back and forth. Our first bet here is $10 and we win. We take back the original bet of $10 plus $5 of the $10 we won, and bet $5 on the second bet. Even if we lose the second bet, we still show a plus $5 for the two hands played. Won one, lost one, but still up $5. It is important to remember that our first bet in this system should be double, or at least more than, the table minimum, because if we win the first bet, we regress to the table minimum to ensure a profit if we lose the second bet. This system is good to use because it is safe during the alternating wins and losses. If you get on a hot streak then, of course, you would add to your bet after each win. How much you add to your bet is always up to you, but I strongly suggest adding only half of what you win and adding the other half to your reserve stack. Remember you are trying to win only $90 as your win goal for the day. A 30 percent return on your investment is a very good return on your money. When a loss occurs in this system, then you revert back to the beginning 2-1-2 betting sequence.

This third betting method is quite similar to the 2-1-2 method, but I prefer this one over it. I came across this method while reading *Progression Blackjack,* a book by Donald Dahl, who in turn got it from a book titled *How to Win,* by Mike Goodman. Thank you both!

This method of progression betting is excellent for my style of play and should be for yours (see Figure 5). It can be used at any level of limits you wish to play to, from $3 to $100 minimum tables. For our scenario with our $300 bankroll and playing at a $10 table (or a $5 table, but making $10 minimum bets), the progression of the bets is 10-10-15-15-20-20-30-30-50-50-70-70-100-100. As you can see, the minimum is $10 and the maximum is $100, or ten times the minimum bet. This method guarantees you that, during your cold streaks, you will lose only the minimum per hand and, during the hot or winning streaks, your chips can stack up pretty fast. As a matter of fact, for us to win our $90 goal, we have to win just six hands in a row. Now I know that winning six hands in a row is a rarity, but with patience, skill, doubling-down, and splitting at the right times, this goal can be reached easier and faster than you might think. This progression style of betting gives you an organized way to reach your goal while protecting your bankroll.

Figure 5

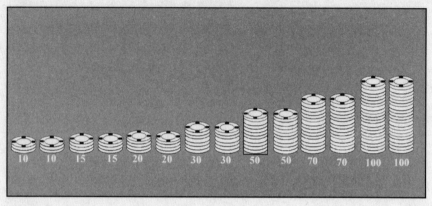

This illustration gives you a visual idea of how fast you can reach the higher betting range using the progressive betting method. There are only two things you need to remember: (1) the "jump" or "skip" rules (see page 63), and (2) when you lose, always revert back to the first betting sequence.

There are faster ways of getting to the big bets with this progression system. For instance, when you get a blackjack and receive the 3 to 2 payoff, you skip one level of betting. To put it another way, let's do this: Suppose on your second $10 bet you get a blackjack and get paid $15. You now skip the first $15 bet and go to the second one. If you split or double-down and win, you can then skip two levels as long as the next bet does not exceed your last payoff. In the event of a loss, you always revert back to the beginning sequence of bets. I think you get the idea behind progression betting methods. Your bankroll, of course, determines what level of progression you would feel comfortable with. You can use it on any table limit and set your own progressions. Just remember that, after a loss, you revert back to the beginning sequence.

Let's get back to our scenario at the casino. There you are, ready to buy in at a table where you feel you will be comfortable playing. You know your win goal is $90 (30 percent of $300), but we haven't talked about a "stop limit." I have mixed feelings about this one. "Stop limits" are important. I don't want you to blow your whole bankroll in one day, but I want you to give yourself every possible opportunity to reach your "win goal." I cannot make these decisions for you, nor will I make them. I am assuming at this point you are an adult and are capable of making rational decisions. Just try to remember this: You are there for only one purpose and that is to win money, to build up that bankroll. I suggest very strongly that when you reach your win goal, in this case $90, you quit for the day. You have been successful by reaching your goal and we are trying to establish a habit of winning. I further suggest that you make a 30 percent "stop limit" on your losses. In other words, if you lose $90, quit for this session. Save that bankroll for another day. I have already said that you won't win every time you play, but man, don't get totally wiped out in any one session. This is just too devastating, not only to your bankroll, but to your self-esteem and your emotions.

As your bankroll grows and your session profits increase, so will your confidence and self-esteem grow. You can do this; it just takes patience and practice. Remember, if you lose the ball, the game is over.

The following are the progression betting sequences as shown on page 43 of *Progression Blackjack,* by Donald Dahl.

$2
2-2-3-3-4-4-6-6-10-10-14-14-20-20
$5
5-5-7-7-10-10-15-15-25-25-35-35-50-50
$10
10-10-15-15-20-20-30-30-50-50-70-70-100-100
$25
25-25-35-35-50-50-75-75-125-125-175-175-250-250
$50
50-50-75-75-100-100-150-150-250-250-350-350-500-500
$100
100-100-150-150-200-200-300-300-500-500-700-700-1000-1000

It is important that you remember and implement these two rules suggested by Mr. Dahl:

1. Upon receiving a payoff of 3 to 2 on a blackjack, skip one level of the progression.
2. Upon winning double or more on the bet, skip two levels unless the money you are risking is more than you just received.

There is another method I would love to share with you concerning winning and money management, but at this time I do not wish to have it published and made public. It is a part of my personal teaching program and is taught at my seminars. Just e-mail me at gphillipcline@ yahoo.com if you want to know more.

18

♥ ♣ ♦ ♠

Percentage Expectation
on
Splitting Pairs

Since the player has no set rules he needs to play by concerning hitting or standing, there are some plays he can make that we call "exotic plays." These consist of splitting pairs and doubling-down. I want to say right up front that I personally am very selective about which of these "exotic plays" I choose to make, and when I make them. You may choose to see it differently than I do. That is your choice.

In most casinos, you are allowed to split any pair (two cards of the same value), making two hands to play instead of one (see Figure 6). Of course, the purpose of this is to get the player to put out more money on the table. This is why timing is so important and why the player should be more selective with these plays. From the player's standpoint, we are trying to make two good hands out of one bad hand. Some pairs, of course, are more advantageous to the player to split than others, depending on the dealer's up card.

In most casinos, the player is also allowed to double-down after splitting a pair (see Figure 7) if he chooses. As far as I am concerned, if you are playing in a casino that won't let you double-down after you have split, the casino is taking advantage of you and you should find another one to play in. Avoid these types of casinos.

Figure 6

Here we are splitting a pair of Aces. I chose to show Aces instead of another pair because of the argument I make against *always* splitting them. I don't think you should *always* split them. The top left hand shows the Aces before we split them. Remember, you get only one card on each Ace when you split them. With any other pair, you can take as many cards as you choose. As you can see, you must make an additional bet the same size as your original one. On the middle hand, we draw an 8, giving us a 19; and on the other Ace, we draw a 3, giving us a 4 or a soft 14. Unless the dealer breaks, we cannot win both hands. The bottom row shows the same hand, but this time we draw our "dream" cards and make two 21s. These are not blackjacks because they are not your original two cards, but they are 21s. In the majority of times that you choose to split Aces, you will win one hand and lose one hand. You will also lose both of them more times than you will win both.

Figure 7

In most casinos, you are allowed to double-down after you split. Here we are splitting 7s. On the first 7 (middle hand), we draw a 3, giving us a total of 10. We chose to double-down on our 10 and we draw an 8, giving us 18. Not too bad. On our second 7, we draw a 4 for a total of 11. We double-down again and draw a 10-count card for a 21. Perfect! We have a good chance of winning both of these hands, but let's look again at what has happened here. What started out as a one-chip bet is now a four-chip bet. We are risking three times more than we originally intended. Anytime you decide to split a pair, you should be committed to going all the way with that decision.

If you are a player who likes to split pairs, fine. I will give you the percentage of expectation on each pair. Let me just remind you that blackjack is a numbers game and not a poker game. Pairs mean nothing except maybe trouble for you if you don't know what you're doing. Always use your head and think before acting on your hand. We are entering that area we talked about earlier where patience, self-control, and money management will make you or break you. When you play smart and lose, that's one thing, but when you play foolish and lose, that's a different-colored horse altogether.

19

Player's Strategy Guide on Splitting Pairs

It is very important that you understand my position on any "exotic" plays, but even more so on splitting pairs. You do not split pairs just because you have them. I do not suggest you split 2s, 3s, or 4s against any up card. I hesitate to say "never," but I have never split 5s against any up card, but simply treat them as any two-card combination that totals 10. I don't split 6s on the theory that I don't want to make two bad hands out of one bad hand. Now 7s through Aces are different, because the percentage expectation of making a good hand is 61 percent. That, plus the expectation the dealer will break, gives credence to doing some splitting. Notice that I don't split 7s against a 2, 3, 8, 9, 10 or Ace. Also, I split 8s only against a 3, 4, 5, 6, 7, or 8; otherwise, I treat the hand as a 16. Split 9s only against a 4, 5, 6, 8, or 9. Stand against everything else.

Now, then, the two 10s. Earlier in this book, I said do not split 10s. You have a good hand and a probable winner. However, under the right conditions, you can justify splitting them. If you do choose to split them, go all the way with them and I mean ALL THE WAY! If you split them, split them to the maximum, up to four times in most casinos. If you catch an Ace to them, *do not* count it as a 21; count it as an 11 and double-down on it. The reasoning is this: You split them in the first place to get all the money you could get on the table in this situation. You must be prepared to go all the way or splitting 10s is a wasted move. If you split them, do so only against the 4, 5, or 6. This play is only for advanced players. Be careful. It is extremely risky.

As you can see in Table 1 (page 75), I treat Aces differently also. You have the same 61 percent chance of making a good hand, the same as with 10s, but here you get only one card on each Ace. It's a different situation. I suggest splitting Aces only against a 2, 3, 4, 5, or 6; otherwise hit the hand—you have a lot of room.

The Guide

If the player splits deuces (2, 2), he has a 39 percent chance of making a good hand of 7, 8, 9, 10, or 11 to draw to, and a 61 percent chance of making a 3, 4, 5, 6, 12, or 13 to draw to. If the player doesn't split deuces, he has a 39 percent chance of making a good hand of 7, 8, 9, 10, or 11 to draw to and the same 61 percent chance of making a 5, 6, 12, 13, or 14 to draw to. The percentage is the same whether or not you split deuces. Since the percentage expectation is the same here, the only real decision you have to make is whether or not you want to risk twice as much on this hand as you originally had planned to.

If the player splits treys (3, 3), he has a 39 percent chance of making a good hand of 7, 8, 9, 10, or 11 to draw to and a 61 percent chance of making a bad hand of 4, 5, 6, 12, or 13 to draw to. If the player doesn't split treys, he has a 39 percent chance of making a good hand of 7, 8, 9, 10, or 11 to draw to, and a 61 percent chance of making a bad hand of 12, 13, 14, 15, or 16 to draw to. Again, the percentage is the same whether you split treys or you don't split them. Same situation, same decision.

If the player splits 4s (4, 4), he has a 39 percent chance of making a good hand of 7, 8, 9, 10, or 11 to draw to, and a 61 percent chance of making a bad hand of 5, 6, 12, 13, or 14 to draw to. If the player doesn't split 4s, he has a 61 percent chance of either making a good hand to draw to (a 10 or 11) or making a good hand of 17, 18, or 19, and a 39 percent chance of making a bad hand of 12, 13, 14, 15, or 16. As you can see, the percentage expectation did a complete reversal in the player's favor. It should be plain to see that the player has the worst of it if he splits 4s.

If the player splits 5s (5, 5), he has a 39 percent chance of making a good hand of 7, 8, 9, 10, or 11 to draw to, and a 61 percent chance of making a bad hand of 6, 12, 13, 14, or 15. If the player doesn't split fives, he has a 61 percent chance of making a good hand of 17, 18, 19, 20, or 21, and a 39 percent chance of making a bad hand of 12, 13, 14, 15, or 16. Again, we see a reversal of percentage expectation by not splitting 55. Unless you have more money than Forrest Gump, don't split 5s.

If the player splits 6s (6, 6), he has a 39 percent chance of making a good hand of 7, 8, 9, 10, or 11 to draw to, and a 61 percent chance of making a bad hand of 12, 13, 14, 15, or 16. If the player doesn't split 6s, he has a 39 percent chance of making a good hand of 17, 18, 19, 20, or 21, and a 61 percent chance of making a bad hand of 13, 14, 15, 16, or breaking with a 22. This is a bad situation. You have the same percentage expectation of making a bad hand if you split or if you don't. You *must* take the dealer's up card into consideration. Since you have the same percentage expectation, there is no reason to split one bad hand and end up with two bad hands. I never split 6s, unless all I'm trying to accomplish is to change the run or flow of the cards, and I have the minimum bet.

If the player splits 7s (7, 7), he has a 61 percent chance of making a good hand of 9, 10, or 11 to draw to or making a good hand of 17 or 18. He has a 31 percent chance of making a bad hand of 12, 13, 15, or 16. If the player doesn't split 7s, he has a 39 percent chance of making a good hand of 17, 18, 19, 20, or 21, and a 61 percent chance of either making a 15 or 16 or breaking the hand. I do recommend splitting 7s, but only against the dealer's up card of 2 through 7, nothing else.

The reason the percentage expectation on splitting 7s and 8s does not add up to 100 percent is that in most casinos you can split up to four times. For example: If the player splits 7s and the next card off is another 7 (giving a total of 14), then if the player could not split them again, we would have to consider that this is a bad hand and figure that into the percentage expectation. However, since you can split them again, and should do so, we can't figure the remaining 7s in the deck as bad cards. We also cannot calculate the 7s as good cards either, so we simply don't count them at all in this situation; therefore, with the uncounted cards, the percentages don't add up to 100. The same is true when splitting 8s and Aces.

If the player splits 8s (8, 8), he has a 61 percent chance of making a good hand of 10 or 11 to draw to or making a good hand of 17, 18, or 19. He has a 31 percent chance of making a bad hand of 12, 13, 14, or 15. If the player doesn't split 8s, he has a 39 percent chance of making a good hand of 17, 18, 19, 20, or 21, and a 61 percent chance of breaking. As you can see, the player is much better off splitting 8s, but only against the dealer's up card of 2 through 8 or an Ace. Not against a 9 or a 10-count card.

If the player splits 9s (9, 9), he has a 61 percent chance of making a good hand of an 11 to draw to or making a good hand of 17, 18, 19, or 20. He has a 39 percent chance of making a bad hand of 12, 13, 14, 15, or 16. If the player doesn't split 9s, he still has a solid play with the 18. If you are the type of player who likes to split pairs, you are going to split them regardless of what I say here. If you must split 9s, at least try to control yourself and split them only against the dealer's up card of 2 through 8 or an Ace. Not against a 9 or a 10-count card.

If the player splits 10s (10, 10), this includes any two 10-count cards because in splitting 10s, they do not have to be identical (see Figure 8). In other words, you may split a 10 and a Jack or a Queen and a King. You can split any two 10-count cards. But why in the wide world of sports would you even consider it? (More on the subject of splitting 10s

Figure 8

Splitting 10s: Do I or don't I? Let's look at it. We are dealt two 10-count cards (top left); they *do not* have to be a pair. We decide to split them. We draw a 4 (top middle), giving us a 14. We decide to stand on it. On our other hand (top right), we draw another 10-count card and have a 20. We can split these again if we choose. We do! On the next hand (bottom left), we draw an Ace. We have a 21, not a blackjack but a 21. On the next hand (bottom right), we draw a 9, giving us a 19. We stand. (We did not double-down on the 21 intentionally in this illustration just to keep it simple.)

What has happened? If the dealer breaks, we win all four hands. If he doesn't break, we will come out only two hands ahead, but we will have risked three times as much as we originally wanted. Was the thrill and the action worth the risk? That is your decision alone to make. Don't blame me if you lose—unless you are willing to give me the credit if you win.

later.) You are holding the second-best hand you can have. Only one other hand will beat it and only one hand will tie it. However, if the player splits 10s, he has a 61 percent chance of making a good hand of 17, 18, 19, 20, or 21. He has a 39 percent chance of making a bad hand of 12, 13, 14, 15, or 16. If the player doesn't split them, he still has a solid 20 to play. As far as I'm concerned, most players who split 10s don't know "giddy-up" from "whoa," and they are splitting them only because they saw someone else do it. This is a valuable hand and you need to know when the time is right to split them.

If the player splits Aces, he has a 61 percent chance of making a good hand of 17, 18, 19, 20, or 21, and a 31 percent chance of making absolutely nothing (see Figure 8). I honestly can't give you a percentage expectation if you don't split Aces because of the vast number of combinations that are possible since you are not limited to drawing one card. The percentage expectation on just one card is a 39 percent chance you will make a good hand of 17, 18, 19, 20, or 21. Of course, if you don't, you are free to keep drawing.

I certainly agree that it's a good bet to split Aces. I just don't think you should split them against a 10-count up card. Remember, you just get one card when you split them. I always play Aces as conservatively as I can. I split them only against the dealer's up card of 2 through 6.

That way, if I don't make a good hand out of them, I still have the possibility of the dealer breaking his hand. Aces just simply are not as great a pair to split as they are cracked up to be since you get only the one card.

In splitting pairs, you must first find out the rules of the casino on splitting. How many times can you split? Can you double-down after you split? When a player does split pairs, he should be committed to going all the way with them and split them to the maximum limit if the opportunity presents itself.

I'm sure you have noticed by now that any pair you split from 2 through 6 has the same percentage expectation of a 39 percent chance of making a good hand to draw to and a 61 percent chance of making a bad hand to draw to. Common sense tells us that when we split 2s through 6s, we are taking the worst of it. This does not mean "don't do it," it just means to be patient and do it when the time is right. Timing is everything in this game of blackjack.

I'm also sure you have noticed the same is true when it comes to splitting pairs of 7s through 10-count pairs, except in reverse. With these pairs the player has a percentage expectation of a 61 percent chance of making a good hand with one card and a 39 percent chance of making a bad hand.

It is you who will decide, when the time comes, how to play your cards or your money. All I am trying to do is to let you know what to expect and what your chances are of making a good hand or a bad one.

If you are a player who likes to split 10-count cards, I hope I wasn't too rough on you for doing so. I enjoy a good gamble myself, but splitting up a total of 20 is just a concept I have a problem grasping. Again, it is a different story if you are prepared to go all the way with the splits—even to the point of doubling-down if you catch an Ace on the 10-count card and count the total as an 11 and not a 21. It may sound as if I'm wishy-washy on this splitting 10s thing. Not really. The situation always dictates what course of action I take. Sometimes yes, sometimes no.

Splitting Aces to me is in a category all by itself. I do not agree with the common theory of always splitting Aces. I just personally do not give the Ace as much power as a lot of folks do. When you get two Aces, it is always tempting to split them at first sight. All I'm saying is if you have observed that a lot of 10-count cards have been played and are out of the deck, think before you split. Use your intuition and observational capabilities before acting on your hand. Again, I think you are doing the right thing if you always split them against the dealer's up card of 2 through 6. When you look down and see a pair of Aces in front of you and you are glad that now you have a chance to "double your fun," by all means split them. On the other hand, if you have an uneasy feeling or feel you can't afford the additional required bet, don't split them. This is intuition. Listen to it. It is your survival kit.

20

Splitting 10s—A Comprehensive Look

Wow! This subject is as controversial to blackjack players as "instant replay" is to football fans. Do we do it or don't we? Yes or no? Hey, guys, it really isn't that simple, or that black and white.

When this subject first came up, I guess I was like most players and thought it was stupid. You would have to be an idiot to split up a 20. A player that does split 10s can clear a blackjack table of players faster than a player who just ate three bowls of chili!

But why? Other than the fact that you are busting up a great hand and might wind up with two or more bad hands, there isn't any difference in splitting 10s or Aces or 8s or 9s when you begin considering the reason why we split pairs in this game to start with. That reason, of course, is simply to get as much money as possible on the table when the dealer is showing a possible weak hand or up card.

I have witnessed two things when I have split 10s, or have seen someone else do it. Other players get visibly angry, sometimes even verbally abusive, and the person doing the splitting usually wins the hand. Let's always keep this in mind: Blackjack is not a "team sport." It may be a group activity, but it's not a team sport.

I will repeat this more than once in this book. Splitting 10s can be profitable if it is done at the right time. Meaning, split them only against the dealer's up card of 4, 5, or 6. Nothing else! Please also keep in mind two things: (1) Once you decide to split them, go all the way with it, and (2) do not think that it is necessary for you to make good hands out of them. Don't be afraid to let the dealer break. By going all the way, I mean just that. If you split 10s and catch another 10, split again to the maximum times allowed. If you catch an Ace to a 10, do not count it as a 21, but as an 11—and double it down. You are trying to get as much money on the table as you possibly can in this situation and at this point. If you win, the other players will congratulate you and say, or think, you are the smartest player they have ever seen. However, ole buddy, if you lose and by your splitting cause the other players to lose, you will be the biggest you-know-what that has ever walked the earth!

We know from percentage expectation on splitting pairs that the chances of your making a good hand by splitting 10s are the exact same chances you have of making a good hand splitting 7s, 8s, 9s, or Aces. So what's the difference? Timing and the reaction and acceptance of other players at the table make the difference.

When talking to other players about splitting 10s, I was surprised to hear that the majority of them do not disagree with the concept of splitting 10s under the right situation and conditions, but they will do it only when playing heads-up with the dealer. In other words, they want to split 10s, but they don't want anyone to see them do it for fear of being labeled a stupid player. Nobody wants to be laughed at.

Do you really want to know why I'm leaning in the direction of splitting 10s? Because in a lot of casinos today they offer instructional classes on the casino games. On every occasion, when I've heard the instructor talk about splitting 10s, he has this to say: Never do it!! If the casinos say never split 10s, that's exactly what I want to do. The reverse is also true—for example, when they say always split 8s, always split Aces. Watch out and pick your splits very carefully.

Summary

There's not much left to say about splitting pairs; we hit this subject pretty hard. I'm sure my critics will have plenty to say about some of the plays I have suggested here. Let me reiterate—I don't care about what they have to say. My only concern here is that after you read this book and try some of my methods for yourself, I want you to be a consistent winner at the blackjack table. Only time will tell if I'm right.

Splitting pairs is an exciting part of this game, but it is only profitable if you win. If you are playing for the fun and excitement of it, split all the pairs you get. You will get a belly full of fun and excitement. But if you are playing to win money, be very selective about splitting. Take your time and think about it.

Table 1

Player's Strategy Guide on Splitting Pairs Using Percentage Expectation

Dealer's Up Card:

	2	3	4	5	6	7	8	9	10	Ace
Player's Hand:										
2, 2	H	H	H	H	H	H	H	H	H	H
3, 3	H	H	H	H	H	H	H	H	H	H
4, 4	H	H	H	H	H	H	H	H	H	H
5, 5	H	H	D	D	D	H	H	H	H	H
6, 6	H	H	S	S	S	H	H	H	H	S

(See Player's Strategy Guide (Chapter 27, page 95) on Total of 12)

	2	3	4	5	6	7	8	9	10	Ace
7, 7	SP	SP	SP	SP	SP	SP	H	H	H	S
8, 8	SP	SP	SP	SP	SP	SP	SP	S	S	SP
9, 9	SP	SP	SP	SP	SP	S	SP	SP	S	SP
10, 10	S	S	S/SP	S/SP	S/SP	S	S	S	S	S

Includes any two 10-count cards

	2	3	4	5	6	7	8	9	10	Ace
A, A	SP	SP	SP	SP	SP	H	H	H	H	H

KEY: H = Hit
  S = Stand
  D = Double
  SP = Split
  S/SP = Stand or Split

21

♥ ♣ ♦ ♠

Percentage Expectation
on
Doubling-Down

In most casinos today, the player is allowed to double-down on any two original cards. Keep in mind, however, that anything a casino will allow a player to do is usually not in the best interest of the player.

To "double-down" simply means the player matches his original bet with a second bet (usually the same-size bet, but some casinos will let you double for less) and receives one card to complete his hand (see Figure 9). Receiving only one card, of course, is the drawback of doubling-down. As a smart percentage blackjack player (and after reading this book you will be), you should pick your spots for doubling-down very carefully. By that I mean doubling-down should not be an automatic play on your part. Just because you have been dealt a 10 or 11 doesn't mean you have to double-down. Just because you see the other players do it doesn't mean you have to. If you double-down and lose, you have to win two single bets just to make up for that one loss. You could find yourself in a hole a coal miner couldn't dig his way out of. I do not want that to happen to you.

Some books say there are times you should double-down on a 7, 8, or 9. I totally disagree with this. If you double on a 7, 8, or 9 and catch a 2, 3, or 4, you are going to feel really stupid for losing your money with a total count of 9, 10, or 11. You will invariably have a blackjack "guru" sitting at your table giving his "expert" advice to every player at the table, especially if the other players are female. I don't care if he has black chips stacked so high he can rest his chin on them, do not double-down on a 7, 8, or 9.

Before you double-down even on a 10 or 11, ask yourself, "Do I really want to do this?" Listen for the answer from that "inner voice." That's your intuition. Listen to it. I can't preach this enough. What a wonderful gift your intuition is. It is your built-in protection.

76

Figure 9

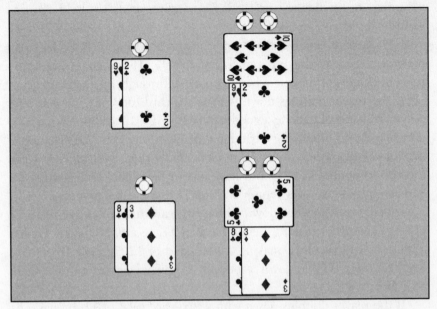

Here are some examples of doubling-down on an 11. In both hands, we have an 11 and choose to double it down. We put up another bet the same size as the original in most cases, although you can double-down for less if you want. Remember, when you double-down, you get only one card. In the top example, we draw a 10-count card for a 21. Great. Same situation in the bottom example, but we weren't as lucky here: we draw a 5 for a 16. Yuck! The dealer will have to break for us to win this one.

Note when you double-down, the card you draw is placed sideways on your original two cards so that the pit boss can just glance at the table and tell what is going on and the surveillance camera can see what is happening.

I am a firm believer in doubling-down only when you have a 10 or an 11, and then only against the dealer's up card of 4, 5, or 6. In other words, only when the player has the percentages in his favor both in doubling-down on his hand and in the possibility of the dealer breaking his hand.

Please don't misunderstand me, I love to gamble and doubling-down is exciting. I just think it is best to do it when you have the percentages in your favor and working for you.

Once again, it's your money and your time. I'm just trying to help you be a winner at this game and I know you can be.

The Guide

If the player doubles-down with a two-card total of 7, he has a 39 percent chance of making a good hand of 17 or 18. He has a 61 percent chance of making a terrible hand of 9 through 16. This is a dumb play, regardless of the dealer's up card. You might as well just hold a gun to your head and rob yourself.

If the player doubles-down with a two-card total of 8, he has a 46 percent chance of making a good hand of 17, 18, or 19. He has a 54 percent chance of making a bad hand of 10 through 16. Don't do it.

If the player doubles-down with a two-card total of 9, he has a 54 percent chance of making a good hand of 17, 18, 19, or 20. He has a 46 percent chance of making a bad hand of 11 through 16. Your chance of making a good hand is over 50 percent, but I don't believe it is worth the risk to double on a 9. You have a zero possibility of making a 21, and you might lose your money with an 11 if you catch a deuce.

If the player doubles-down with a two-card total of 10, he has a 61 percent chance of making a good hand of 17, 18, 19, 20, or 21. He has a 39 percent chance of making a bad hand of 12 through 16. This is your optimum double-down, especially if utilized against an up card of 4, 5, or 6.

If the player doubles-down with a two-card total of 11, he has a 61 percent chance of making a good hand of 17, 18, 19, 20, or 21. He has a 39 percent chance of making a bad hand of 12 through 16. Again, the optimum opportunity for you, if you take advantage of it against the 4, 5, or 6 up card.

If the player doubles-down with a two-card total of 12 through 16, he has a 39 percent chance of making a good hand of 17, 18, 19, 20, or 21. He has a 61 percent chance of going from the frying pan right into the fire. As a matter of fact, if you double-down on a 12 through 16, you can call in the dogs and pee on the fire because it is just a matter of time before you are broke.

Summary

As you can see, the player has the best chance of making a hand when he doubles-down with a two-card 10 or 11. The percentage expectation is identical with these two numbers. Combine that percentage with the dealer's percentage expectation for breaking his hand with an up card of 4, 5, or 6—which is 46 percent, 54 percent, or 61 percent, respectively—and you have an excellent shot at winning this hand. I know that most of you will find this hard to do, just because of the temptation to double anytime you are holding a 10 or 11 against any up card. However, if you double only against an up card of 4, 5, or 6, you will win more hands, make more money, and your ability to demonstrate self-control, patience, and money management will greatly improve.

I want to emphasize one thing about doubling-down with a 12 through 16: If you are a player who doubles-down on these numbers, neither this nor any other book will be able to save you from losing your money. All I can say is, you must have one helluva good job.

22

Hitting and Doubling-Down
on *Soft-Count* Hands

In all my playing and observation of this game, the hands that seem to be the most confusing and cause the player the most problems are the soft hands.

A "soft" hand in blackjack is one that contains at least one Ace in it, and when the Ace is counted as 1 the hand cannot be broken by any one card. For some reason, a lot of people get confused when it comes to counting a soft hand.

I have found the easiest way to count a soft hand is to count the Ace as 1, add the value of the other card to it, and add 10 more. For example, if you are holding A, 5 (see Figure 10), you count the hand as 6 and mentally add 10 to it. Your hand is 6 or soft 16. Since there isn't a card in the deck that will break a hand of 6, you would naturally take a card. Let's say you catch a 10-count card when you hit. Your hand is now A, 5, 10, or 16. Now there are a lot of cards that will break a 16, so you have more decisions to make. Let's say you have the same hand of A, 5 and you take a hit and catch a 4. Your hand is now A, 5, 4; 1 plus 5 is 6 plus 4 is 10 plus 10 is 20. Your hand is now 10 or a soft 20. Another example: Your hand is A, 7. You count the Ace as 1 plus 7 is 8 plus 10 is 18. Your hand is 8 or a soft 18. With just a little practice you will feel comfortable in counting any soft hands that may come up (see Figure 11).

Many players like to double-down on soft hands. There are certainly some good opportunities that come up during a playing session that can be profitable for you to double-down on. However, I am still sticking to my conservative approach on doubling with a soft hand. This may cause you to think that I'm not much of a gambler, but no one can deny I am a damn good card player, and I will walk away more times a winner than

Figure 10

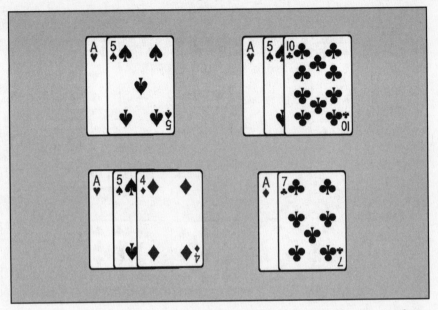

This example is again on soft hands. You are dealt an Ace, 5 (top left), giving you a 6 or soft 16. You hit and draw a 10-count; you now have a hard 16. (This hand can be broken by drawing another card.) Bottom left hand, the same Ace, 5 and you hit again, but this time you draw a 4, giving you a 10 or soft 20. Normally, you will stand on a 20. Bottom right hand is a simple Ace, 7 for a total of 8, or a soft 18.

not. I double-down on soft hands only against the dealer's up card of 4, 5, or 6. The following information will give you your percentage expectation on doubling-down on soft hands. Remember, when you double-down, you get only one card, so you can't afford to make any mistakes.

If the player doubles-down with an A, 2 (3 or a soft 13), he has a 39 percent chance of making a good hand of 17, 18, 19, 20, or 21. He has a 61 percent chance of making a bad hand of 4, 5, 6, 12, or 13. As you can see, you have the worst of it if you double-down on this hand, and yes, I see players do it all the time. Sure, you will win some of them, but you will lose the majority of these bets.

If the player doubles-down with an A, 3 (4 or soft 14), he has a 39 percent chance of making a good hand of 17, 18, 19, 20, or 21. He has a 61 percent chance of making a bad hand of 5, 6, 12, 13, or 14. Same deal here. There are better places to risk your bankroll.

If the player doubles-down with an A, 4 (5 or soft 15), he has a 39 percent chance of making a good hand of 17, 18, 19, 20, or 21. He has

Figure 11

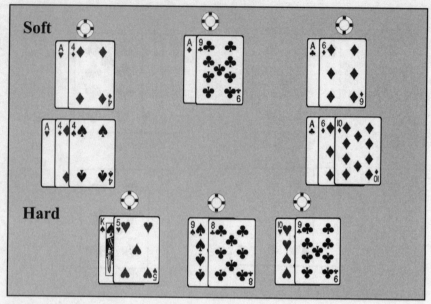

If you are still confused about the difference between a "soft" and a "hard" hand, this figure will illustrate the difference once more.

Top row left to right: Ace, 4 is a soft 15. You cannot break it with any card in the deck. You draw a card and catch another 4; you now have a soft 19 and stand.

Top middle, Ace, 9 is a soft 20. No one card can break it, but it is a 20. If at any time you want to hit this hand, *double it down* as a 10 and take one card to it. If you do decide to double-down on this hand, please do so only against a 4, 5, or 6.

Top right is a soft 17; middle right is a hard 17; middle left is a soft 19; bottom left is a hard 15; bottom middle is a hard 17; and bottom right is a hard 19. Just remember: A soft hand cannot be broken by drawing an additional card and contains at least one Ace in it. A hard hand can be broken by drawing an additional card.

I hope this helps clear up any confusion.

a 61 percent chance of making a bad hand of 6, 12, 13, 14, or 15. Do you see a pattern?

If the player doubles-down with an A, 5 (6 or soft 16), he has a 39 percent chance of making a good hand of 17, 18, 19, 20, or 21. He has a 61 percent chance of making a bad hand of 12, 13, 14, 15, or 16. Same old thing here too. Save your money.

If the player doubles-down with an A, 6 (7 or soft 17), he has a 61 percent chance of making a good hand of 17, 18, 19, 20, or 21. He has a 39 percent chance of making a bad hand of 12, 13, 14, 15, or 16. Ah! Now look what's happened. The percentages are now in our favor and we can do some serious thinking about doubling-down. That does not mean it is an automatic course of action. Think about it before you act. Again, only against a 4, 5, or 6 up card, please.

If the player doubles-down with an A, 7 (8 or soft 18), he has a 61 percent chance of making a good hand of 17, 18, 19, 20, or 21. He has a 39 percent chance of making a 12, 13, 14, 15, or 16. An 18 is not that bad of a hand, soft or hard, but in the right situation there is money to be made by doubling-down on this hand. Pick your spots carefully.

If the player doubles-down with an A, 8 (9 or soft 19), he has a 61 percent chance of making a good hand of 17, 18, 19, 20, or 21. He has a 39 percent chance of making a bad hand of 12, 13, 14, 15, or 16. Same situation here. You have a good hand, but depending on the dealer's up card, you could pick up an extra bet here.

If the player doubles-down with an A, 9 (10 or soft 20), he has a 61 percent chance of making a good hand of 17, 18, 19, 20, or 21. He has a 39 percent chance of making a bad hand of 12, 13, 14, 15, or 16. You are holding a hand of 20, a hand that can be beat only by a 21. Still, under the right circumstances, you can make an extra bet. Definitely only against a 4, 5, or 6.

If the player doubles-down with an A, 10 (11 or soft 21), a blackjack, a natural 21 that pays 3 to 2 on your bet, he has a 61 percent chance of making a good hand of 17, 18, 19, 20, or 21. He has a 39 percent chance of making a bad hand of 12, 13, 14, 15, or 16. He also has a 100 percent chance of being crazy. If anyone at your table doubles-down with a blackjack, get your butt up and move. This last statement is a bit extreme. You really don't have to move tables, but at least make a mental note that this person is not playing smart blackjack.

When you are holding A, 2 through A, 5, you have only a 39 percent chance of making a good hand. Why risk twice as much by doubling-down?

When you are holding A, 6 through A, 9, you have a 61 percent chance of making a good hand. That high percentage, coupled with the high percentage that the dealer has of breaking, makes this an attractive proposition. The decision of doing so is left entirely up to you; therefore, you can stand or double-down. The one exception is the combination of A, 6, or soft 17. Never stand on this hand. Either hit it or double it, but don't stand on it.

Summary

The exotic play of doubling-down on a soft-count hand can add some excitement and profit for a player who knows how and when to do it. As you can see, when doubling-down on an A, 2 through A, 5, the percent-

Table 2

Player's Strategy Guide on Soft-Count Hands

Dealer's Up Card:

Player's Hand:	2	3	4	5	6	7	8	9	10	Ace
A, 2	H	H	H	H	H	H	H	H	H	H
A, 3	H	H	H	H	H	H	H	H	H	H
A, 4	H	H	H	H	H	H	H	H	H	H
A, 5	H	H	H	H	H	H	H	H	H	H
A, 6	H	D	D	D	D	H	H	H	H	H
A, 7	H	D	D	D	D	S	S	S	S	S
A, 8	S	S/D	S/D	S/D	S/D	S	S	S	S	S
A, 9	S	S	S/D	S/D	S/D	S	S	S	S	S

KEY: H = Hit
         S = Stand
         D = Double
         S/D = Stand or Double

age expectations are all the same and all against the player's chances of making a decent hand. That's why I think it is poor playing to double-down on these hands. However, if the dealer's up card is a 4, 5, or 6, it can be fun and profitable to do it because of the percentage expectation of 46 to 61 percent that the dealer will break his hand.

Again, you can see that when the player doubles-down with an A, 6 through A, 10, the percentage expectation completely reverses itself with the percentages in the player's favor of making a good hand. Add that to the dealer's chances of breaking with an up card of 4, 5, or 6, and it is plain to see why many players will take the risk and double-down on soft-count hands.

Some casinos, will allow a player to double-down on a natural black-jack. Why not? It would certainly be in their favor for you to do it, and believe it or not, some people will. Let's say you have $10 bet and you get a blackjack. You automatically get paid 3 to 2 or $15. If you double-down, you have to put out another $10, and *if* you get lucky and win the hand, you get paid even money. You are laying 2 to 1 odds on the second bet instead of taking the 3 to 2 odds on a sure thing. Not smart!

23

♥ ♣ ♦ ♠

Is Blackjack Skill or Luck?

How many times have you heard someone say, "I would rather be lucky than good any day"? I hear it almost every day, and there have been many days when I know I was playing my very best, but I was still losing. I just didn't have any good luck that day.

Luck certainly plays a big part in the game of blackjack, as it does in every gambling game.

The problem with luck is that it's not very reliable, while skill is. If you play every blackjack hand the very best way you know how to play it, luck will eventually fall in and follow.

The two go hand in hand and make a great combination. As a matter of fact, on those rare occasions when you have both of them working for you, you are unbeatable.

Yet, it is ironic that at times you can't win with skill only, but you can win with luck only. I've seen it happen many times, as I'm sure you have. For example, I was sitting on third base playing an absolutely brilliant game of blackjack, but still losing my ass off, when up staggered Al K. Holic and his beautiful daughter; at least, I think she was his daughter.

Anyway, Al started fumbling around for his money while muttering to the dealer that he sure would like a cold one. Al sat down, which surprised me because I didn't think he even knew there was a chair there. I thought about moving, but I was comfortable where I was and I didn't think Al would last long with the $40 he bought in with.

Well, three hours and a dozen cold ones later, I was down $400 and Al, with his head on the table, had $100 chips stacked up higher than his beer can. The man could do no wrong. He played just about every hand wrong. He split when he shouldn't have, he doubled-down on 12s and 13s; he hit stiff hands against the dealer's up cards of 5 and 6. The cards were literally running over his butt and he was drunker than a peach orchard boar. However, my God, he was lucky. He was winning over $5,000 and couldn't hold his head up.

As luck will, she left without saying goodbye, and an hour and a half later Al K. Holic didn't have a chip left and I managed to get close to even. As Al was leaving the table, one of his friends asked him, "How did you do?" Al calmly muttered, "I lost $40." End of story.

I told this story only to show you that things usually work out better when you have a combination of both ingredients of skill and luck.

Now, please don't interpret this to mean you have to get drunk to get lucky. Nothing can be farther from the truth. As a matter of fact, I've found the more skillful I become, the luckier I get.

24

♥ ♣ ♦ ♠

Cheating

Does cheating exist in casinos today? I honestly do not know the answer to this question. Furthermore, does the question mean, do the casinos cheat the players or do the players cheat the casinos? I don't know.

You know, it is very hard to write about something after you have admitted or said I don't know. I can only state my opinions on this subject and I don't mind doing that.

Let me say a few words about me. I am a card player exclusively. I don't shoot craps, I don't play roulette, and I don't play the slots. I play blackjack and poker, but mostly blackjack. When it comes to putting my money on the table, I suddenly get very aware of the environment around me. I become very suspicious of everyone and everything in that environment, even to the point of paranoia at times. This is a habit that grew out of playing in private games where there was some big money involved. I have been cheated on several occasions in poker games, and once in a big blackjack game. I have observed some other games that I had been invited to for the purpose of watching, just so I could report back to some of the players on whether or not they were being cheated. They were. I am not going to go into the many methods used to cheat in private card games because that would be a book in itself. Besides, for our purpose it really isn't important because we are talking about public gambling in this book, and not private gambling.

Let's be realistic and honest with ourselves here and say that cheating is just as possible in public as it is in private, but not as probable.

I am happy to say that, as far as I know, I have never been cheated in a public casino. Of course, the big part of that statement is, "as far as I know." I have many times been the victim of some very poor "floor decisions" made by some very poor "floor managers" who ruled in favor of the casino, but was I cheated? At the time I certainly thought so, but when you accuse someone of cheating, you need to know for sure you were cheated and not just think so.

If casinos are cheating today, the cheating would be so sophisticated that we, as players, would never see it. If you get cheated in public casinos today, it is something you feel, not something you see.

When you see a big winner who's been sitting at the same blackjack table for hours, sitting in the same chair, playing with the same dealer who still has two hours to deal before her shift ends, but when her break is over, she is sent to the roulette table and a different dealer replaces her at the blackjack table that she has been dealing at all day, and the new dealer comes in and even with the same cards has this ungodly run of good cards and takes the big winner's chips and more besides, have you just witnessed a player being cheated? It is very possible you have. The player who was the big winner most certainly thinks so.

I have seen the above scenario so many times I can't count them. But was the player cheated? Moving the "cold" dealer to another table and replacing her with a "hot" dealer was a deliberate managerial decision that was made to get the casino's money back from the player. But was it cheating?

I have never heard of a casino changing dealers when a player gets "hot" on the dice table, so why do they do it on a blackjack table?

Let's not kid ourselves here—there are dealers who can do whatever they want to with a deck of cards and you can't see them do it. Even when they tell you in advance what they are going to do, you still can't see it. Blackjack shoes can be rigged so the dealer can "peek" at the card and deal that card or the next one (this is called dealing seconds), depending on which one is needed.

Let's be real on this subject. Sure it can be done, but casinos aren't going to cheat you in any way that can be picked up by surveillance cameras, or use anything tangible like marked cards or a rigged shoe that can be seized and used as hard evidence against them in court by a player complaining to the State Gaming Commission.

Like I said, even if you are being cheated, you won't see it. You will feel it, but you won't see it.

Protect yourself as best you can against cheating. Stay away from hand-held decks being dealt by dealers who use "jerky" hand movements, or who hold the deck up by their chests or chins. These are typical moves of a card "mechanic" and totally unnecessary in an honest game. Don't play with these dealers. You will probably get a "straight" game anyway, but why risk it?

I love to watch a dealer shuffle the cards; I don't mean I have a fetish about it, but I like to see what's going on. Have you ever noticed that these new shuffling machines have dark glass doors that close when the decks are being shuffled? You can't see what's going on in there. What the heck is so secretive about shuffling decks of cards if everything is on the up-and-up? Makes you wonder, doesn't it? Are we being cheated in some way?

That's a deal, isn't it? The casinos hire a dealer, send her to dealing school for four to six weeks to teach her how to shuffle that particular casino's house shuffle, and to teach her procedures about the game of blackjack. In other words, they teach her how to deal the game, then they put her on the casino floor, pay her minimum wage, then pay $10,000 or a monthly rental fee for a shuffling machine. Makes you think the shuffle is more important to this game than the dealer or knowing how to deal it. Is the shuffle important to a blackjack game? You better believe it. Is it possible to be cheated by a systematic shuffle done by a machine behind closed dark glass doors? Is it possible for a man to leave Florida or Texas and in a few days be walking on the moon? Is it possible to "clone" a sheep? Is it possible to take the heart out of one human being and place it successfully in the chest of another? Now let me ask you again: Is it possible for a shuffling machine to "stack" several decks of cards so that the cards are rigged against the players? You're a smart person, you tell me.

Possibility versus probability. The debate will go on forever. We, as human beings, like to trust and to be trusted; these are values that make up our character. If you "think" you are being cheated in a casino, it is probably just because you are losing. However, if you "feel" like you are being cheated, that feeling can hit you even when you are winning. Should you ever get that "feeling," don't question it, simply cash out your chips and leave.

It is only fair to talk about the other side of the coin—players who try to cheat the casino. I detest any kind of cheating in card games. I don't even like the word, but what I can't stand the most is a card cheat's stupidity. Man, you have to be an idiot to think you can cheat a casino over a period of time. Sure, you can try to "cap" your bet (add more chips to your bet when you have a good hand) or "drag" your bet (take chips off your bet when you have a bad hand), but you are stupid to think you can get away with it. There are surveillance cameras everywhere, and unless you know where the blind spots are and even if the dealer is in with you, you will get caught. In most states a player caught cheating in a casino is charged with a felony.

I have seen players take a payoff from a dealer who has made an honest mistake and they really think they have gotten away with something. This tells me about that person's character. But is it cheating? Yeah, I think it is. Dealers can and do make mistakes and overpay; don't take it, give it back. It's all on tape. Besides, it will make you feel better about yourself.

In one book about blackjack, I couldn't believe what I was reading. The author was actually advising the reader to do this: "If you are hitting a breaking hand and catch a card that breaks you by one, giving you a 22, act excited and say something like, 'Oh boy, a 21, let's see you beat that.'" He was saying, in essence, that if you do that, the dealer might make a mistake and pay you anyway. This author, this so-called blackjack expert, was telling his readers to cheat. I couldn't believe it. This guy has no honor or integrity.

If you, as a player, see anyone cheating at the table you're at, get away from there. Tomorrow morning when you are shaving—or, you ladies, when you are combing your hair—you can look at yourself in the mirror and still like *you*.

25

Spanish 21

This is the only variation of blackjack I will write about in this book, and the only reason I even mention it is I want the new players to the world of casino action to stay away from this money pit.

Besides the standard rules for conventional blackjack, the game of Spanish 21 has added some very attractive side rules and bonuses:

1. If a player and the dealer both have a blackjack (a push in conventional blackjack), the player wins and receives the standard 3 to 2 payoff.
2. When the player's hand totals 21, he is paid off even if the dealer makes a 21.
3. You may split any pair up to three times for a total of four separate hands, and you can double-down after splitting.
4. You may double-down and receive one card at any time, even after taking a hit; in other words, after three or four more cards, you can double-down.
5. Get this one: After you double-down, if you don't like your hand, you may withdraw your double and surrender the original bet.
6. If you have a hand that totals 21 and it is made up of a 6, 7, and 8, you receive a bonus of 3 to 2, 2 to 1, or 3 to 1. This depends on whether the 6, 7, and 8 are of different suits, all the same suit, or all spades.
7. A hand that totals 21 and is made up of five, six, or seven cards pays 3 to 2, 2 to 1, and 3 to 1, respectively, while a hand totaling 21 and made up of more than seven cards pays off at 3 to 1.
8. If the player's original hand consists of three 7s (dealt two 7s and then hits for the third 7), the payoff is again 3 to 2, 2 to 1, or 3 to 1,

again depending whether they are made up of different suits, all the same suit, or all spades.

9. Now this one will really get you! The casinos that I've been in where Spanish 21 is played give an added bonus if you receive three 7s, all in the same suit, while the dealer is showing an up card of 7. This bonus will range from $1,000 to $5,000, depending on how much the player has bet. If he has bet $5, the bonus is $1,000. If he bets $25 or more, his bonus is $5,000. Wait a minute, there's more! If the player who is holding this hand has bet $25 or more, every player at the table receives a bonus of $50 each.

Now, with all this going on, why do I not want you to play it? Literally speaking, if you play Spanish 21, you aren't playing with a full deck! All the 10s have been removed from the decks, leaving only the Jacks, Queens, and Kings as 10-count cards.

Since Spanish 21 is played with six decks from a shoe, that's twenty-four 10s that have been removed. As conventional blackjack players, we should know by now how important 10-count cards are to the player and why you should not play this game. If you are on a riverboat and run into this game and have an urge to play it, this is what you should do. Go to the top deck of the boat and throw your money into the river. This way at least you have a chance that the current of the river will carry your money to the riverbank and maybe you'll find it on the way home!

26

♥ ♣ ♦ ♠

Let the Dealer Break

Our time together is getting short. I truly hope I haven't bored you with this percentage stuff. If I did, you aren't alone—I get bored writing about some of it too. I never get bored playing the great game of blackjack. It is always an interesting challenge.

I would like to remind you to "Let the Dealer Break." Folks, this is very important to your wallet. Since you have to act on your hand first, of course your money is always in jeopardy; that's part of the game and part of the excitement of playing it. But don't just sit there breaking hand after hand, and giving your money away. "Let the Dealer Break." Stand pat on some of those stiff hands against the dealer's 10-count up cards and "Let the Dealer Break"; at least give her a chance to break.

When I was a young man, I sold cookware door-to-door to single working gals for their hope chests. (Some of you may not even know what a hope chest is.) The company I worked for had a slogan that I have used over the last twenty-five years in several aspects of my life, and it fits in well in playing blackjack. The slogan in abbreviated form was "SIBKIS." It stands for "See It Big, Keep It Simple." That slogan still works for me today. Don't be afraid to "See It Big," but since we aren't Einsteins, let's "Keep It Simple." "Let the Dealer Break." If I could give you only one piece of advice about this great game, that would be the one. Now this does not mean never hit a stiff hand. In no way will that work. All it means is, "You Must Stay in the Hand to Win It." Even as great a player as Michael Jordan was, he couldn't score from the bench. You can't either, so once in a while, "Let the Dealer Break."

27

♥ ♣ ♦ ♠

The Player's Strategy Guide

Explanation

It has been suggested that I include in this book a copy of the traditional basic strategy guide so the readers can compare the two guides and the two strategies. I have decided not to do this. The main reason is that my strategy is very easy to commit to memory and very easy to use. I do not want to confuse, or in any way hamper, my readers by presenting another strategy, which is, as far as I'm concerned, obsolete.

Table 3, on the other hand, presents the player's strategy guide based on percentage expectation. In brief: I want my readers to hit when they have a total of 9 or less. Do not double-down on a 7, 8, or 9. I do not want you losing your money on a hand that totals 11 or less. Double-down on a 10 or 11, but only against an up card of 4, 5, or 6. Everything else on this table should be self-explanatory.

Table 3

Player's Strategy Guide

Dealer's Up Card										
	2	3	4	5	6	7	8	9	10	Ace
Player's Total										
9 or less	H	H	H	H	H	H	H	H	H	H
10	H	H	D	D	D	H	H	H	H	H
11	H	H	D	D	D	H	H	H	H	H
12	H	H	S	S	S	H	H	H	H	S°
13	H	S	S	S	S	H	H	H	H	S°
14	S	S	S	S	S	H	H	H	H	S
15	S	S	S	S	S	S	S	S	S	S
16	S	S	S	S	S	S	S	S	S	S
17	S	S	S	S	S	S	S	S	S	S
18	S	S	S	S	S	S	S	S	S	S
19	S	S	S	S	S	S	S	S	S	S
20	S	S	S	S	S	S	S	S	S	S
21	S	S	S	S	S	S	S	S	S	S

H = Hit
S = Stand
D = Double

°This advice is based on a blackjack game in which the dealer hits a soft 17. If the dealer stands on a soft 17, hit your 12 and 13 against the up card of an Ace.

28

♥ ♣ ♦ ♠

Closing Remarks

Regardless of what method or system you use, to be successful playing blackjack you must have and must put into practice all the discipline, self-control, and money management you can gather up, and then reach down inside yourself and find some more. You must believe that you are a good blackjack player and that the method you are using works for you. You must stay mentally focused on your play and your goals.

If you choose to play blackjack by percentage expectation, remember that the whole idea is to take as much gamble out of the game as you can. Double-down on a 10 or 11, but only against a 4, 5, or 6. Split only pairs that are 7s or higher and then only against a 4, 5, or 6 for the optimum expectation. If you don't remember what the percentage expectations are after reading this book, read it again, *and again*, until you know them from memory. Memorize the Player's Strategy Guide (Chapter 27, page 95) to the point that you know exactly how to play every hand (even though you won't play the same way every time).

After reading this book and playing by percentage expectation, you should be winning one to three hands more per shoe than you won before you read it. If you are doing that, this book has fulfilled its purpose.

Keep in mind that no matter what method you use or how good you are as a blackjack player, or think you are, you must have Lady Luck on your side once in a while. I can't tell you how to get lucky, but I have found that the more knowledge you have about the game, and the smarter you play, the luckier you become. If you are playing at a table where Lady Luck seems to be on the side of the dealer, move to another table. That combination is too hard to beat. I have discovered that Lady Luck is something of a whore. She'll sleep with you one night and someone else the next, but whore or not, you better respect this lady.

Use your intuition and first impulses to your advantage. Your intuition is usually right for your best interest. Remember that blackjack is just a game and you should have fun playing it. If you play it right, you can make money and have an enjoyable time, too.

After reading this book, you should know when to hit and when to stand, when to double-down and when not to, when and what to split and when and what not to. If you still have questions, e-mail me at gphillipcline@yahoo.com, or look me up on the net at www .professional-blackjack.com.

29

♥ ♣ ♦ ♠

A Blackjack Quiz

In Figure 12, I show two similar double-down situations for the third-base position. If I was the player playing this position in the top example, I would not double-down on this 11. I have talked throughout this book about doubling-down an 11 against a 4, 5, or 6 and yet I would not double in this situation. Why?

The bottom example is very similar, but quite different indeed. Even though the dealer's up card is a 10-count card, I would not hesitate to double-down this 11. Why?

I said at the beginning of this book that I hope to make a thinking blackjack player out of you and that nothing is an automatic course of action.

Think about these two "whys." If you don't fully understand the "whys," e-mail me at gphillipcline@yahoo.com and let's talk about making you a winner at this game.

If you are interested in becoming a professional blackjack player, visit me at www.professional-blackjack.com. Let's talk!

Figure 12. Matt's Missing Link.

30

Problem Gamblers

Millions of people gamble. Some of them are social or recreational gamblers, and some are professional gamblers. Some are compulsive, some are quite controlled, and some are addicted.

All of them can be problem gamblers at some time or other. The possibility is always there. A very thin line separates these types of gamblers, and it's a line that can be crossed easily.

If you, or anyone you know, is a problem gambler, or even think they might have a problem with gambling, please find help. Problems can be solved. You owe it to yourself and your loved ones. Please contact:

The National Council on Problem Gambling, Inc.
1-800-522-4700

Always Good Luck,
G. Phillip Cline

APPENDIXES

A.

Possible Two-Card Combination Totals

(When Playing with Six Decks)

How many ways can you make a 21 with two cards?
(A, 10) = 24 possible ways

How many ways can you make a 20 with two cards?
(A, 9; 10, 10) = 72 possible ways

How many ways can you make a 19 with two cards?
(A, 8; 10, 9) = 48 possible ways

How many ways can you make an 18 with two cards?
(A, 7; 10, 8; 9, 9) = 60 possible ways

How many ways can you make a 17 with two cards?
(A, 6; 10, 7; 9, 8) = 72 possible ways

How many ways can you make a 16 with two cards?
(A, 5; 10, 6; 9, 7; 8, 8) = 84 possible ways

How many ways can you make a 15 with two cards?
(A, 4; 10, 5; 9, 6; 8, 7) = 96 possible ways

How many ways can you make a 14 with two cards?
(A, 3; 10, 4; 9, 5; 8, 6; 7, 7) = 108 possible ways

How many ways can you make a 13 with two cards?
(A, 2; 10, 3; 9, 4; 8, 5; 7, 6) = 120 possible ways

How many ways can you make a 12 with two cards?
(10, 2; 9, 3; 8, 4; 7, 5; 6, 6) = 108 possible ways

How many ways can you make an 11 with two cards?
(9, 2; 8, 3; 7, 4; 6, 5) = 96 possible ways

How many ways can you make a 10 with two cards?
(A, 9; 8, 2; 7, 3; 6, 4; 5, 5) = 108 possible ways
(A, 9 should be counted as 20)

How many ways can you make a 9 with two cards?
(A, 8; 7, 2; 6, 3; 5, 4) = 96 possible ways
(A, 8 should be counted as 19)

How many ways can you make an 8 with two cards?
(A, 7; 6, 2; 5, 3; 4, 4) = 84 possible ways
(A, 7 should be counted as 18)

How many ways can you make a 7 with two cards?
(A, 6; 5, 2; 4, 3) = 72 possible ways

How many ways can you make a 6 with two cards?
(A, 5; 4, 2; 3, 3) = 60 possible ways

How many ways can you make a 5 with two cards?
(A, 4; 3, 2) = 48 possible ways

How many ways can you make a 4 with two cards?
(A, 3; 2, 2) = 36 possible ways

How many ways can you make a 3 with two cards?
(A, 2) = 24 possible ways

How many ways can you make a 2 with two cards?
(A, A) = 12 possible ways

WAYS TO MAKE A TWO-CARD COMBINATION FOR A:

```
 2 = 12 ways
 3 = 24 ways
 4 = 36 ways
 5 = 48 ways (24 not counting A, 4)
 6 = 60 ways (36 not counting A, 5)
 7 = 72 ways (48 not counting A, 6)
 8 = 84 ways (60 not counting A, 7)
 9 = 96 ways (72 not counting A, 8)
10 = 108 ways (84 not counting A, 9)
```

11 = 96 ways (not counting A, 10)
12 = 108 ways
13 = 120 correct ways (96 not counting A, 2)
14 = 108 ways (84 not counting A, 3)
15 = 96 ways (72 not counting A, 4)
16 = 84 ways (60 not counting A, 5)
17 = 72 ways
18 = 60 ways
19 = 48 ways
20 = 72 ways
21 = 24 ways

There are 420 possible ways to make a two-card stiff hand as compared to only 276 possible ways to make a two-card pat hand. The result is that there are 144 more ways to make a stiff hand than a pat hand. You have a 21 percent chance of being dealt a pat hand (17, 18, 19, 20, 21), a 33 percent chance of being dealt a stiff hand (12, 13, 14, 15, 16), and a 46 percent chance of being dealt a hand that is neither a pat hand nor a stiff hand (2, 3, 4, 5, 6, 7, 8, 9, 10, 11 or soft 13, 14, 15, 16).

B.

Percentages of Two-Card Stiff Hands

A stiff hand is any two-card combination that totals 12 through 16, not counting soft hands.

(12)
(10, 2; 9, 3; 8, 4; 7, 5; 6, 6)
Ways to make a stiff 12 = 108 ways
Cards that improve it to a 17, 18, 19, 20, 21 = 120 cards or 39 percent
Cards that break it = 96 cards break it or 31 percent
Cards that don't make or break it = 96 cards or 31 percent

(13)
(10, 3; 9, 4; 8, 5; 7, 6)
Ways to make a stiff 13 = 96 ways
Cards that improve it to a 17, 18, 19, 20, 21 = 120 cards or 39 percent
Cards that break it = 120 cards or 39 percent
Cards that don't make or break it = 72 cards or 22 percent

(14)
(10, 4; 9, 5; 8, 6; 7, 7)
Ways to make a stiff 14 = 84 ways
Cards that improve it to a 17, 18, 19, 20, 21 = 120 cards or 39 percent
Cards that break it = 144 cards or 46 percent
Cards that don't make or break it = 48 cards or 15 percent

(15)
(10, 5; 9, 6; 8, 7)
Ways to make a stiff 15 = 72 ways
Cards that improve it to a 17, 18, 19, 20, 21 = 120 cards or 39 percent
Cards that break it = 168 cards or 54 percent
Cards that don't make or break it = 24 cards or 8 percent

(16)
(10, 6; 9, 7; 8, 8)
Ways to make a stiff 16 = 60 ways
Cards that improve it to a 17, 18, 19, 20, 21 = 120 cards or 39 percent
Cards that break it = 192 cards or 61 percent

These figures will vary depending on the combinations of cards used, but the percentages are accurate within 1 percent. I am using all 312 cards and am not allowing for the dealer's up card or any set number of players. This is just to give you an overview of the situation.

C.

Percentage Strategy

DEALER'S UP CARD IS A 2:

When the dealer's up card is a 2, there is a 39 percent chance (120 cards) of him having a good hand to draw one card to (7, 8, 9, 10, 11), while only a 31 percent chance (96 cards) of drawing to a breaking hand.

YOUR HAND:

9 or less—hit until you have 15 or better
10—hit until you have 15 or better
11—hit until you have 15 or better
12—hit until you have 15 or better
13—hit until you have 15 or better
14—stand
15—stand
16—stand

DEALER'S UP CARD IS A 3:

When the dealer's up card is a 3, there is a 39 percent chance (120 cards) of him having a good hand to draw one card to (7, 8, 9, 10, 11), and a 39 percent chance (120 cards) of drawing to a breaking hand.

YOUR HAND:

9 or less—hit until you have 15 or better
10—hit until you have 15 or better
11—hit until you have 15 or better
12—hit until you have 15 or better
13—stand
14—stand
15—stand
16—stand

DEALER'S UP CARD IS A 4:

When the dealer's up card is a 4, there is a 39 percent chance (119 cards) of him having a good hand to draw one card to (7, 8, 9, 10, 11), and a 46 percent chance (144 cards) of him drawing to a breaking hand.

YOUR HAND:

9 or less—hit until you have a 12 or better
10—double
11—double
12—stand
13—stand
14—stand
15—stand
16—stand

DEALER'S UP CARD IS A 5:

When the dealer's up card is a 5, there is a 39 percent chance (119 cards) of him having a good hand to draw one card to (7, 8, 9, 10, 11), and a 54 percent chance (168 cards) of him drawing to a breaking hand.

YOUR HAND:

9 or less—hit until you have 12 or better
10—double
11—double
12—stand
13—stand
14—stand
15—stand
16—stand

DEALER'S UP CARD IS A 6:

When the dealer's up card is a 6, there is a 39 percent chance (120 cards) of him having a good hand to draw one card to (7, 8, 9, 10, 11), and a 61 percent chance (191 cards) of him drawing to a breaking hand.

YOUR HAND:

9 or less—hit until you have 12 or better
10—double
11—double
12—stand
13—stand
14—stand
15—stand
16—stand

DEALER'S UP CARD IS A 7:

When the dealer's up card is a 7, there is a 61 percent chance he is pat or drawing to a good hand, and a 39 percent chance he is drawing to a breaking hand.

YOUR HAND:

9 or less—hit until you have 15 or better
10—hit until you have 15 or better
11—hit until you have 15 or better
12—hit until you have 15 or better
13—hit until you have 15 or better
14—hit until you have 15 or better
15—stand
16—stand

DEALER'S UP CARD IS AN 8:

When the dealer's up card is an 8, there is a 61 percent chance he is pat or drawing to a 10 or 11, and a 39 percent chance he is drawing to a breaking hand.

YOUR HAND:

9 or less—hit until you have 15 or better
10—hit until you have 15 or better
11—hit until you have 15 or better
12—hit until you have 15 or better

13—hit until you have 15 or better
14—hit until you have 15 or better
15—stand
16—stand

DEALER'S UP CARD IS A 9:

When the dealer's up card is a 9, there is a 61 percent chance he is pat or drawing to an 11, and a 39 percent chance he is drawing to a breaking hand.

YOUR HAND:

9 or less—hit until you have 15 or better
10—hit until you have 15 or better
11—hit until you have 15 or better
12—hit until you have 15 or better
13—hit until you have 15 or better
14—hit until you have 15 or better
15—stand
16—stand

DEALER'S UP CARD IS A 10:

When the dealer's up card is a 10, there is a 61 percent chance he is pat, and a 39 percent chance he is drawing to a breaking hand.

YOUR HAND:

9 or less—hit until you have 15 or better
10—hit until you have 15 or better
11—hit until you have 15 or better
12—hit until you have 15 or better
13—hit until you have 15 or better
14—hit until you have 15 or better
15—stand
16—stand

DEALER'S UP CARD IS AN ACE:

When the dealer's up card is an Ace, there is a 31 percent chance he has a blackjack, a 23 percent chance he is pat, and a 46 percent chance he is drawing (if dealer is hitting a soft 17).

YOUR HAND:

9 or less—hit until you have 12 or better
10—hit until you have 12 or better
11—hit until you have 12 or better
12—stand
13—stand
14—stand
15—stand
16—stand

Do not hit a breaking hand against an Ace (unless the dealer is standing on a soft 17). *See The Player's Strategy Guide (Chapter 27, page 95).

These figures and percentages are based on one card showing only. Of course, these would change in actual play depending on the cards showing. This is just to give you an overview of the strategy.

D.

Table 4

Percentage Information on Dealer's Up Card

	What are the chances the down card will produce a pat hand of 17, 18, 19, 20, 21	What are the chances the down card will produce a one-card draw to a good hand of 7, 8, 9, 10, 11	What are the chances the down card will produce a one-card draw to a breaking hand of 12, 13, 14, 15, 16	What is the percentage that the dealer has to draw at least one card
If up card is:				
Ace	168 cards/54% (not counting soft 17)	7% 6s only	0%	46%
10 count	191 cards/61%	0%	120 cards/39%	39%
9 count	167 cards/54%	24 cards/7% 2s only	120 cards/39%	46%
8 count	144 cards/46%	48 cards/15%	119 cards/39%	54%
7 count	120 cards/39%	72 cards/22%	119 cards/39%	61%
6 count	0% not counting soft 17	120 cards/39%	191 cards/61%	100%
5 count	0%	119 cards/39% not counting Aces/7%	168 cards/54%	100%
4 count	0%	119 cards/39%	144 cards/46%	100%
3 count	0%	120 cards/39%	120 cards/39%	100%
2 count	0%	120 cards/39%	96 cards/31%	100%

GLOSSARY

Backing Up Cards

(A) The dealer "backs up" a hand to "prove" it in case of a question about the hand. To "back up" a hand, the dealer retrieves the cards from the discard rack and replaces them in correct order as picked up from the players.

(B) To move cards from one hand to another (not allowed in most casinos); again in case of a mistake.

Bankroll

(A) Casino chips (checks) kept in a tray in front of the dealer (Table Bankroll).

(B) A player's money that has been allocated for gaming (Player's Bankroll).

Barber Pole

A stack of chips (checks) in different denominations and in random order.

Base (First, Second, or Third)

Player's position at the table. First base is to the dealer's far left. Second base is the middle spot (sometimes called centerfield). Third base is the last position to the dealer's far right.

Blackjack

An Ace and any 10-count card received on the original two cards dealt to the player or the dealer. Payoff is 3 to 2.

Break

To exceed a total of 21; also called "bust."

Burn

To take one or more cards out of action by putting them face down in the discard holder.

Capping

Placing additional chips (checks) on top of the original bet when you think it is a winner. (This is illegal in most states and can land you in jail.)

Chips/Checks

Monetary units issued by the casino in exchange for cash. Each color has a different cash value.

Clean Money

Casino checks that are taken out of the tray and used to pay off winning bets.

Cold Turkey

A hand that totals 20 in the original two cards.

Convert

To exchange lower-value chips for higher-value chips; also called "color up."

Count

(A) To keep count as to what cards have been dealt and what cards remain in the deck.

(B) Total value of a hand.

Crimp

A crease or bend on a card that makes it easy to identify.

Cut Card

(A) A colored plastic, nonplaying card that indicates when it is time to shuffle.

(B) The card used to cut the deck by the player.

Dealer

The person who deals the cards at a blackjack table.

Dirty Money

Losing bets collected by the dealer. Never used to pay off another player's winning bet.

Discard Holder

A plastic box on the right corner of a blackjack table used to stack already played cards.

Double-Down

To make a second bet equal to or less than the original bet. The bet is placed *behind* the original bet. When doubling-down, the player receives only one additional card. When your second bet is less than your first bet, it is called doubling for less.

Dragging

To reduce a bet by removing chips/checks before the cards are dealt. (This is legal.) If you reduce your bet or "drag" after the cards are dealt, it is illegal.

Drop Box

A box hanging under the table where cash and documents are placed.

Even Money

A term used for a payoff to a player holding a blackjack when the dealer is showing an Ace as an up card.

Hard Total

A hand whose total can exceed blackjack by drawing another card.

Heads-Up

One player playing against the dealer.

Hit

To draw additional cards to a hand in order to improve it.

Hole/Down Card

The dealer's second card dealt face down and placed under the first card.

Insurance

An optional bet made by the player that the dealer has a "blackjack." This bet may be made only when the dealer's up card is an Ace. The bet may not exceed one-half of the original bet. The payoff is 2 to 1.

Intuition
The immediate knowing or learning of something without the conscious use of reasoning; instantaneous apprehension.

Lay-Out
The cover on top of a blackjack table, usually green and usually felt. It shows players' betting positions, etc.

Money Management
The protecting of your bankroll. A *must* to be successful.

Natural/Snapper
A blackjack in the original two cards dealt. An Ace and a 10-count card. A blackjack!

Nausea
The feeling you get when the dealer makes a miracle draw-out and beats your pat 20.

Pat
Not drawing additional cards.

Pat Hand
A hand that totals 17, 18, 19, 20, or 21 in the original two cards dealt.

Peeking Device
A device used to determine the dealer's hole card.

Pinch
To illegally take chips/checks from a bet after cards have been dealt.

Pips
The spots on a card, e.g., the 5 of Clubs has 5 pips.

Point Count
The total value of the hand.

Push/Stand Off
A tie between the dealer and the player. Neither one wins, and no money changes hands.

Scratch
The physical signal asking for a hit (additional cards).

Shoe
The device used to hold the cards while dealing.

Shuffle
A mixing of the cards.

Soft Hand
One that includes an Ace that can be counted as 1 or 11 without exceeding the point count of 21.

Spanish 21
A variation of traditional blackjack.

Split Pairs
Making two hands out of one when the first two cards are of equal value. The original bets must be duplicated, and the bet is placed *beside* the original bet.

Stand
Not to take any additional cards.

Stiff
A hand in which the value of the first two cards total 12 through 16 and, therefore, could break by drawing one more card.

Toke/Tip
A gratuity given to the dealer.

Up Card
The dealer's card that is showing face up.

BIBLIOGRAPHY

Braun, Julian H. *How to Play Winning Blackjack*. Chicago: Data House Publishing, 1980.

Dahl, Donald. *Progression Blackjack*. New York: Citadel Press, 1993.

Goodman, Mike. *How to Win*. Ingram Publishing, 1992.

Humble, Lance. *Blackjack Supergold*. Toronto: International Gaming, 1979.

Revere, Lawrence. *Playing Blackjack as a Business*. New York: Citadel Press, 1994.

Silberstang, Edwin. *Winning Blackjack for the Serious Player*. New York: Cardoza Publishing, 1993.

Thorp, Edward O. *Beat the Dealer*. New York: Random House, 1966.

Uston, Ken. *Million Dollar Blackjack*. New York: Barricade Books, 1995.

ABOUT THE AUTHOR

Mr. Cline was born in Kansas City, Missouri, where he also grew up. He attended Missouri Western State College in Saint Joseph, Missouri.

He has played poker and blackjack for a living since 1972. He is single and has three children—two sons and a daughter.

He currently makes his home in San Angelo, Texas.

Figure 13

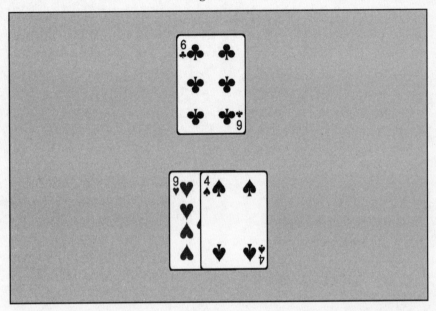

For you people who look at the last page first: If you don't know how to play this hand of blackjack, you should start reading this book from the first page. You are probably playing blackjack backward too. This book will help with your blackjack play, but won't break you of the habit of looking at the last page first.